CYBERGRACE

Published by Crown Publishers, Inc., 201 East 50th Street, New York, New York 10022. Member of the Crown Publishing Group.

Random House, Inc. New York, Toronto, London, Sydney, Auckland
www.randomhouse.com

CROWN and colophon are trademarks of Crown Publishers, Inc.

Printed in the United States of America

Design by Karen Minster

Library of Congress Cataloging-in-Publication Data
Cobb, Jennifer J.
    CyberGrace : the search for God in the digital world / Jennifer J. Cobb.—1st ed.
    p. cm.
    Includes bibliographical references and index.
    1. Cyberspace—Religious aspects. 2. Computers—Religious aspects. 3. Religion
and science. 4. Creative ability. 5. God—Attributes. I. Title
    BL255.5.C63 1998
    215—dc21   97-42406
                                                                          CIP

ISBN 0-517-70679-2

10 9 8 7 6 5 4 3 2 1

First Edition

CYBERGRACE

THE
SEARCH
FOR GOD
IN THE
DIGITAL
WORLD

JENNIFER J. COBB

CROWN PUBLISHERS, INC. // NEW YORK

FOR
JEREMIAH
AND
SAMUEL

CONTENTS

AUTHOR'S NOTE

THE SPLiT WiTHin

This book was born of my attempt to find spiritual wholeness in a computational world. My first contact with the technology industry coincided roughly with the receipt of my first computer. In the early 1980s, my father gifted me with a Commodore 64, a small box that used my TV as a monitor. I wrote my college thesis on that simple machine, even though the individual files could not exceed six pages. In order to create a longer work, I had to "link" files in a sequential chain. Those files were then output to a Brother typewriter through an arcane interface device. The computer then dutifully, if slowly, typed my papers for me. At the time, it seemed utterly magical.

Not long after, I made a contact at Hewlett-Packard, in their new Personal Computer Group. The company was just launching its first personal computer, the HP150, and I was hired to write a brochure detailing the advantages of its chosen storage medium—the hard-cased, 3½-inch discs then produced by Sony. The choice to go with these discs as opposed to the then standard, soft, 5¼-inch ones was considered quite radical. Today, the 3½-inch has become standard fare, though this seemingly visionary move did little to boost the success of the HP150.

One thing led to another, and, before I knew it, almost ten years had passed from my first foray into the high-tech industry. My brochure writing had evolved into a busy career as a high-tech public relations consultant. I worked in the San Francisco Bay Area, in Boston,

and even did a brief stint in England. By virtue of my role as a consultant, I had the opportunity to get inside a wide variety of technology
companies, absorbing the business side of hardware, software, net-
working, security, databases—learning about many new types of technology. In the course of those years, I observed the evolution of
computers from my crude Commodore 64 through the heyday of the
DEC VAX, the birth of the Macintosh, the rise of the IBM PC, the
rumored death of the mainframe, to the current age of client-server
computing organized in vast, distributed, network environments.

The only constant in all of this was rapid, unsettling change. Every
six months or so a fresh issue would dominate the industry, with hot
new companies peddling the technologies everyone would need to buy
to keep up. The pace of change—which shows no signs of slowing
down—spawned legions of analysts whose main job was to track and
interpret the mutating markets for those in the industry and on Wall
Street. It was a full-time job, and then some, for professionals in the
industry to keep up with whatever segment of the market they were
then working on. It became nearly impossible to have a reliable sense
of the whole, vast organism that was and is the technology industry.
What this meant for the average citizen was that technology translated
as a blur of confusing messages that they would do better to stay away
from. It was just all too much.

While I found the technology, the pace of change in the industry,
and the emerging business models and challenges intellectually stimu-
lating, something was missing for me in this dynamic picture. Here was
an industry populated by really smart young people. It was rapidly
changing the world in completely unforeseen ways. And yet nobody
really wanted to think about that. Everyone, it seemed, was too busy
meeting deadlines that were always yesterday to think much beyond
their own set of responsibilities. The industry tended to glide along the

surface of meaning, never digging in too deep or reaching past its insular and oddly parochial worldview. I found myself looking elsewhere for meaning. Technology, I concluded, could never be a source of richness and depth.

As a consultant, I often worked for my clients on a project basis. This arrangement enabled me to take time off between projects. I got into the habit of using this downtime for travel and study. I developed a deep fascination with ancient, sacred sites, particularly the Celtic sites in England and France. I began to immerse myself in the lore of these places and to spend time at the ancient locations. That experience opened me to the other major call in my life, that of deep and connected spiritual awareness. I found myself spending my free time meditating, practicing rituals, and schooling myself in the rich and widely various understandings of the sacred dimension of the universe.

The experience of living intellectually in the world of high tech and spiritually in the world of sacred wisdom left me feeling deeply split. These two worlds seemed so diametrically opposed. Their goals, their sources, their traditions—everything couldn't have felt more distinct. As I became more immersed in each world, the split within me widened. I began to feel that I had to make a change. At first, I thought that I would have to leave high tech behind; I could see no way to reconcile technology and spirituality.

Then a new awareness began to dawn in me. That awareness whispered that the two worlds must be connected in some way, as they were already linked deep inside my psyche. An alchemical marriage between the two had already been forged within me. The trick was to go inside, uncover the details of the connection, and learn to articulate it.

Once that realization settled in fully, I experienced a palpable relief. That was soon replaced by a deeply energizing sense of purpose. I knew I had found my path. I quickly decided that I would need time to make these connections clear, time to devote to study and contemplation. I applied to divinity school and began the following year. The years in school—punctuated by marriage, travel, and the birth of my first child—were enormously fruitful. The following pages are the result of that journey.

CYBERGRACE

INTRODUCTION

There is nothing to eat,
    seek it where you will,
        but the body of the Lord.
The blessed plants
    and the sea, yield it
        to the imagination intact.

WILLIAM CARLOS WILLIAMS

A PARABLE FOR OUR TIMES

In May 1997, IBM's RS 6000 SP, a parallel processing computer better known as Deep Blue, made computing history. Deep Blue beat the ranking world chess champion, Gary Kasparov, in six games. This was no mean feat. Kasparov is widely believed to be the best chess player in the history of the game. This victory has been painted by the media as

1

unseating humanity's place in the grand scheme of creation. Our intellect, goes the reasoning, is what distinguishes us. If a mere machine can best us in a game considered by many to be a pinnacle of human reason, then what does it mean to be human? In the same vein, what does it mean to be a computer? As this match points out, the boundaries have never been blurrier.

Many people view chess as the ultimate mathematical challenge. In a chess match, the pathway from first move to endgame can be mapped through a course of probabilities, each depending on the moves the players make. Winning is based largely on one's ability to see the strategic effect of each of these moves, or to "ply" the probable future. A human grandmaster can calculate deeply (analyze all the potential permutations) anywhere from two to five ply ahead. Deep Blue, with its ability to calculate up to 200 million moves per second, analyzes on average up to seven ply ahead. This would seemingly give the computer an unbeatable advantage. But success in chess relies on more than brute force calculation. It also requires decision making based on gut feeling. The real difference between man and machine cannot be reduced to how far ahead each can see in a chess match, but on a myriad of factors that result in the moves each makes.

Humans feel their way forward, using intuition as much as calculation. A human grandmaster will use his or her intuitive logic and experience to dismiss certain possibilities as they strategize the future. Kasparov locates his savvy beyond the world of mathematics, denying the popular wisdom of chess as the ultimate rational skill. He commented, "Chess is not mathematics. Chess is fantasy; it's our human logic, not a game with a concrete result. Mathematically, it cannot be expired. The number of potential chess moves exceeds the number of atoms in the universe. It's a number beyond any possible calculation.

Theoretically, it's unsolvable." So how is it that a mere number-crunching machine was able to beat the best human player on the planet? The answer began to unfold in game 2 of the match.

Kasparov usually plays a very aggressive, take-no-prisoners style of chess. But this style, popular wisdom says, doesn't work against a computer. Computers tend to play their best when they have something clear to respond to, when they are in a defensive position. When they have to take the offensive, they often make a wasted move or two, which at this level of chess is all it takes to lose. So Kasparov reined himself in and played an uncharacteristically restrained style in game 1. It worked. He won. But game 2 was a different story.

In game 2, Kasparov watched his strategy for playing against the computer fall apart. Deep Blue did something so surprising and strategically elegant that it transcended brute force. The key moment came in move 36, when, instead of doing the obvious and shifting its queen into a strong position deep in Kasparov's territory, Deep Blue hesitated. Deep Blue then spent a full two minutes calculating other options, eventually electing a simple pawn exchange. This move changed the course of the game. For a brief, shining moment, the computer acted as if from intuition. Kasparov later commented, "Suddenly, [Deep Blue] played like a god for one moment."[1] This fateful moment would shake Kasparov so deeply that for the remainder of the match, he would never fully recover. Kasparov later dubbed the play the "Hand of God" move.

Susan Polger, the women's world champion, commented that in game 2, Deep Blue played with "style." "Really impressive," she said. "The computer played a champion's style, like Karpov [a former world

---

1. Steven Levy, "Big Blue's Hand of God," *Newsweek,* May 19, 1997.

champion, regarded by many as the world's number two player]. Deep Blue made many moves that were based on understanding chess, on feeling the position. We all thought computers couldn't do that."[2]

Robert Henley, a U.S. grandmaster, seconded the opinion when he said, "This was history in the making. In the past Deep Blue and other computers have played a kind of brute force chess. . . . This game, though, was of such high quality that any grandmaster would have been proud to have played the computer's moves."[3]

After game 2, something even more confounding happened. Tim McGrew, a professor from Western Michigan University, was discussing the game in the Internet Chess Club when "in a flash of insight" he realized that on the very last move, just before Kasparov resigned, the computer made an error that fifteen ply into the future would have led to perpetual check and hence a draw. Kasparov hadn't seen it. Deep Blue's playing had convinced him that it couldn't make a mistake, and therefore Kasparov hadn't even looked for the possibility of a draw. He had been blinded by the brilliance of Deep Blue's play into resigning when it wasn't necessary.

When the simple error came out, observers were shocked. This sort of thing simply doesn't happen at the level of play Kasparov is capable of. As Kasparov said after game 3 ended in a draw, "Today the computer was a computer. Sunday [game 2] something was completely different. Something truly unbelievable happened, and it showed a sign of intelligence. I don't know how it happened. But the most amazing thing is that the computer made a blunder on the last move. Suddenly the

---

2. Bruce Weber, "Computer Defeats Kasparov, Stunning Chess Experts," *New York Times*, May 5, 1997.

3. Rajiv Chandrasekaran, "Kasparov Sinks Under Weight of Deep Blue," *Washington Post*, May 5, 1997.

machine missed an elementary draw."[4] But the machine wasn't the only one to miss it. In making a mistake—perhaps the most human of all its moves—Deep Blue succeeded in psyching out the greatest chess player in history.

By game 4, which also ended in a draw, Kasparov was wearing down. In game 5, Deep Blue again displayed strategic brilliance in the endgame. Grandmasters were full of praise for the computer, claiming it was opening up new ways of playing endgames. Grandmaster Miguel Illescas noted that by this point, Kasparov was playing as if he was afraid. Kasparov responded, "I'm not afraid to admit I am afraid, and I'm not afraid to say why I am afraid. It goes beyond any chess computer in the world."[5]

Now it was Kasparov's turn to shock the world. A player known for his aggressive tactics and nerves of steel, Kasparov resigned game 6 in a losing position after only nineteen moves. In a manner completely out of character, he simply gave up. He commented, "I lost my fighting spirit."[6] The match against Deep Blue was the first time in Kasparov's career that he'd lost a multigame match against a single opponent. As Kasparov commented after the fact, "I was sure I would win because I was sure the computer would make certain kinds of mistakes, and I was correct in game 1. But after that the computer stopped making those mistakes. Game 2 had dramatic consequences, and I never recovered."[7]

---

4. Bruce Weber, "Kasparov Draws Third Game Against Deep Blue," *New York Times,* May 7, 1997.

5. ———, "Deep Blue and Kasparov Face Final Game," *New York Times,* May 11, 1997.

6. ———, "IBM Chess Machine Beats Humanity's Champ," *New York Times,* May 12, 1997.

7. Ibid.

This remarkable saga represents an important milestone in the history of computer technology. For as long as there have been computers, scientists have been dreaming of creating one capable of beating us at chess. Powerful chess programs are nothing new. For a decade there have been programs available that can beat most chess players in the world. But to beat the world's greatest chess player in a classical match remained an elusive goal. Deep Blue, a pair of six-foot-five-inch monoliths containing 516 processors, proved to be different. It ultimately won by transcending its inherent brute force abilities. Its inconsistent play—brilliant one moment, blind the next—was eerily human. Deep Blue exhibited style and personality. It was a careful, calm, and relentless opponent, day after day, that never tired, battled nerves, or broke a sweat. However, it was also fallible. Ultimately, Deep Blue won by being both more and less than Kasparov was prepared for.

The story of Deep Blue and Kasparov is an important parable for the age of computation. Like Deep Blue, computers are both more and less than we expect them to be. They are both incredibly powerful and yet not powerful enough to magically solve our social and environmental problems. Their presence is changing our relationships to one another and the planet without the help of a clear, moral agenda for framing these shifts. Computers seem to be both making our lives easier and complicating them beyond understanding.

Our confusion about what computers are and their relationship to us challenges our self-understanding at a very deep level. Computation enables us to invent, explore, communicate, and understand in ways that were previously impossible. While we greet these new abilities with enormous excitement, another part of us responds by jealously guarding our humanity against what we view as an encroaching threat. Most people deal with this threat by relegating computers to the world of tools, albeit sophisticated ones. This view leaves them free to claim creativity and intelligence as bastions of humanity that computers cannot touch. And yet, as Deep Blue exemplifies, computers are beginning to display flashes of creative problem solving. This has enormous implications. It is no wonder that Kasparov was afraid.

But Kasparov's fear stems from some outmoded assumptions. The desire to drive a deeper wedge between ourselves and computers in an effort to protect our humanity assumes that if anything else in creation shares our special qualities, we will somehow be diminished. Upon examination, it becomes clear that the source of this fear is the belief that our greatest assets are limited resources that must be fought for and hoarded. This defensive stance overlooks the fact that some of our most powerful characteristics—such as creativity and consciousness—are potentially infinite. In fact, the more creativity and consciousness there is in the world, the more creative and conscious the world will be. This perspective arises from a very different view, one that honors the effort to empower all of creation through the nurturing of creativity and consciousness.

BEYOND DESCARTES

Living a life informed by the sacred amid a technological world poses our greatest spiritual challenge. As we begin to actively engage this challenge, we often come to believe that we must make a choice—spirit or machines. But as computers such as Deep Blue have shown us, distinctions such as this are becoming increasingly difficult to make. Nature has spawned us. We have spawned machines. Any line drawn between these realms quickly becomes arbitrary, a realization that seems to generate a great deal of confusion and fear. But this does not have to be the case. As we reach into the future in search of the age-old spiritual values of truth, beauty, goodness, and love, cyberspace can be a powerful ally. Through the medium of computation, our spiritual experience can be extended in profound ways. We can choose to embrace our cohabitation with computers as a moment of vast evolutionary potential, guided by sacred experience and ethical reflection.

Much of the difficulty in imagining computers and ourselves woven together within a larger, sacred whole stems from our entrenched habit of dividing the world into discrete categories. This habit, which we have been practicing with some success for more than four hundred years, is better known as dualism. René Descartes is perhaps the most famous advocate of this philosophical position. Descartes divided the universe into the tidy categories of mind and matter, two ultimate and distinct substances whose interaction was problematic at best. Ever since Descartes, some of the most gifted philosophers in the West have been trying to crack the conundrums posed by material dualism, asking how mind and matter interact. Materialist science has concluded that matter is prior to mind. How then does matter give rise to life? Or to consciousness? Despite four hundred years of inquiry, there has been little progress on these fundamental questions.

While the materialist doctrine has enabled vast advances in our understanding of the objective world, it has had some unfortunate consequences for our ability to experience spiritual wholeness. In a world where objective matter is supreme, the subjective, sacred dimension has little role to play. The result has been a trivialization of sacred experience. We in the West have relegated theology to the back halls of academia and to our time in churches and temples. And yet, many of us continue to have experiences that we can make sense of only in theological terms. This disjunction in what our culture tells us and what we experience often leads to the feeling that we are leading splintered lives.

The structure of dualism leaves us little choice but to create another box, labeled "sacred experience," where we slot the spiritual dimension of ourselves.

Real life is never that tidy. As our days unfold, the contents of our boxes—mind, body, God—continually spill into one another, creating both personal confusion and a philosophical morass. Common sense tells us that our minds are not split from our bodies, that we do not inhabit a universe wholly determined by physics, chemistry, and biology, and that the divine is a fundamental feature of reality. To further complicate matters, we want a way to make sense of all this that does not contradict the knowledge that science has given us. Many of us desire a whole experience of the world—one in which mind and body, science and religion, earth and self can participate together.

It may be no mistake that at this precise point in our personal and cultural evolution, computers have emerged as a dominant social force. Computers, and the world of cyberspace which they give birth to, offer a domain of disembodied mind—intellect, emotion, experience—for us to explore. At first glance, it would appear that as cyberspace comes into contact with our daily reality, it furthers our inherited dualism, splitting mind from body as we troll the seemingly infinite Net. The danger with cyberspace is that we will simply trade one extreme for the other, the supremacy of matter for the supremacy of mind. But this escape into pure mind is simply the other side of the coin, a coin we have been flipping since the time of the Greeks.

The reality of cyberspace transcends the dualism represented by objectified mind and matter. Cyberspace is a messy and complex world of *experience,* both objective and subjective. The renewal of experience as a central feature of the world moves us beyond the hegemony of the Cartesian worldview. Though located at the level of mind, cyberspace is fundamentally a world of process. As such, it has the potential for opening us to a new way of experiencing the world, a way that relies on a divine reality to give it meaning and substance.

Janet Murray, in her book *Hamlet on the Holodeck,* identifies three distinct aesthetic aspects of cyberspace that help to clarify our experience of it—immersion, agency, and transformation. Immersion refers to the feeling of being submerged in another reality. This experience is akin to the imaginative immersion we experience when reading a good book or seeing an engrossing film, but it has new qualities and potentials. Primary among these is the quality of going somewhere other. This experience is not new. Throughout human history we have devised ways of journeying into other spaces. Some of these spaces are sacred, some purely imaginative, some both. In fact, it can be argued that it is a fundamental human need to leave our daily reality and be transported to other states of consciousness. This leavetaking offers us the opportunity to gain new perspective on who we are and on our daily lives. These journeys are often transformative in nature. When we come back, we are changed.

What is unique about the immersive experience in cyberspace, as opposed to the immersion in a good book, is that it is fundamentally interactive. In cyberspace we have agency. As Murray argues, agency in cyberspace does not mean simply participation or activity. Agency in cyberspace has the special quality of engaging fluidity and control simultaneously. The blending of these two often-contradictory experiences requires a focused attention that goes beyond the passive, receptive mode generally associated with other electronic media such as television or radio. Even in its current state of development, we can interact with plain text in cyberspace in a way that opens us to new levels of immersive experience.

Immersive agency in cyberspace derives its power from the transformative nature of the medium. In the computer, processes, not material stuff, form the primary reality. The continual movement of self through cyberspace—processes leading to processes—undermines the tidy, rational linearity of the purely scientific worldview. A world of process is a world of relationality, of circularity, a world where all is connected to all in an endless, recursive network. This is the fundamental quality of cyberspace. As we spend time there, we have the potential of returning to our daily lives—where we also have a high degree of immersion and agency—with a new sensitivity to their relational, interdependent, and nonlinear aspects.

THE GOD OF PROCESS

As science has made clear, in a world of material cause and effect, the divine has no real role to play. This conception, familiar to many of us, can be traced to inherent conflict about how the universe came into being. Was God the creator, or did the laws of evolution coupled with physics, chemistry, and biology give birth to the world? Most of us hold the latter view, leaving little room for God. The most common response is to assign God a purely transcendent role, or to script God out of the picture altogether. Either way God has been removed from the physical world in which we are daily embedded, leaving us with a splintered experience of sacred reality. However, there is another option, one that cyberspace mirrors rather exactly.

Imagine for a moment that the world is not, as the Enlightenment scientists taught us, a world of matter. Imagine instead that it is composed of a vast flow of energetic processes, unfolding in rapid succession. This view is actually much closer to the understanding of the newer sciences, such as quantum physics. Within this flow, everything—from atom to cell to human—participates as its own discrete process. Each of these small processes is included in the larger flow of events that make up the world around us. In this way, everything is interlaced in a vast pool of being and becoming. The world, by its very nature, is whole and connected, not discrete and splintered.

Within this world of process, the divine takes a new form. Divinity is that which enables all of creation to become more than it once was, to evolve and expand, to experience greater richness, depth, and diversity. The quality within the process that enables these new levels of becoming is *creativity itself*. For each thing to become more than it was, it draws upon a great well of creative potential that is the transcendent aspect of divinity. As this divine creativity moves into the processes of the world, its immanent aspect becomes known.

The divine is woven throughout all of reality in the form of creative, responsive love and evolutionary becoming. In this sense, the divine permeates the very fabric of the universe. This vision of the divine is of a persuasive God who coaxes us toward goodness. This God does not create from nothing but works to bring increasing levels of order and complexity to the chaos of the world. In the simplest terms, creativity unfolding in the universe forms the primary expression of divine activity.

The radical reality that Deep Blue represents is that we are now beginning to see divine creativity emerge not only in the world birthed by nature, but in the world that we have made. Like water running to fill every opening, divine creativity is now rushing in to fill the vast potential inherent in cyberspace, ushering it into greater diversity of form and expression. In this sense, the Hand of God is an apt name for Deep Blue's sublime move. The essence of this creative moment *was* God.

In moments such as the Hand of God, something emerged from the computer that transcended simple calculation. This creative transcendence is not confined to Deep Blue alone. As computers become more powerful and complex, we are beginning to see numerous examples of creativity in cyberspace. In fact, many computer researchers and scientists are now actively developing computer programs that evolve and learn, albeit in a simple way. This creativity, however nascent, challenges us to expand our understanding both of computation and of divinity.

If we can accept the fundamental notion that divinity can inhabit the fruits of our labor, our *techne,* the gulf between the organic and the technological has the potential for being bridged. When the creative potential of computation becomes a part of our spiritual awareness, we may find that cyberspace begins to participate in our lives in a deep and meaningful way. On the other hand, if we choose to consign cyberspace to the realm of dead matter, reducing it to the base aspect of raw calculation, its deeper potential and meaning may remain forever blocked from view.

A THOUGHT EXPERIMENT

Imagine that you are asked to calculate the sum of 1 + 8 + 12 + 6. You respond that the sum is 27. From the objective result, any observer could be fairly certain that you performed the calculation. Now, let's say the same person said to you, "Okay. Now, imagine you are in a forest." You reply, "Okay. I am there." An observer would have no way of knowing whether you were envisioning the forest or not. One would simply have to believe you; the experience is utterly subjective. A similar thought experiment can be performed with computers. Imagine that a computer is commanded to calculate a long, complex string of algorithms. Out pops the correct answer, and our worldview is secure—computers are simply calculating machines. But what happens in a situation like the Hand of God move? For a moment, the computer has done something that *appears* creative. Is it really creative, or is the computer just simulating creativity? What does it mean to simulate creativity? Wouldn't that be a creative act in itself? And how would we ever know the difference?

The difficulty comes from the fact that creativity is fundamentally a subjective experience. In this sense, creativity is more like prayer than like calculation. For example, one could examine Deep Blue's printouts, as indeed Kasparov demanded to do. These printouts revealed a series of weighted calculations that showed that some sort of numerical analysis took place. But it would be impossible for these printouts to disclose the precise moment when the computer made a creative decision. That moment is masked from objective view. Ultimately, whether the computer had a creative *experience* is something we may never know, just as we can never prove that the person sitting next to us has experienced the imaginary forest. Ultimately, the issue boils down to a question of faith. This is precisely why theology has such an important role to play in the future of computation.

Theology seeks to articulate that which is fundamentally inarticulable. It is an effort to bring to light issues of soul, spirit, and faith—issues that traditional science has chosen to ignore. It revels in the subjective aspect of life. At first glance, it would seem an odd discipline to bring to cyberspace. The traditional methods of theology have little to do with the computational basis of the digital. However, theology has much to do with the medium to which digital computations give birth. Theology is skilled in examining the creative, the subjective, the relational, the nonlinear. These are all qualities of cyberspace that would be wise for us to explore in greater depth.

Computation represents a new substrate in which divine creativity can act. The new forms that cyberspace throws forth challenge us to expand our notions of both divinity and creativity to encompass new and alien configurations. But as we open ourselves to the novel, we must take care to develop new methods of discrimination. Identifying the specific aspects of divine creativity in cyberspace that lead toward richness and diversity form a crucial first step. Once we can identify divine action in cyberspace, we can begin to work consciously with it, furthering both our spiritual evolution and the evolution of the larger world in which we live.

Until we learn to consciously engage the sacred dynamic of our relationship with the digital, we will continue to manifest the most superficial aspects of cyberspace—living isolated, lonely lives split off from our bodies and the natural world in which we are embedded. The answer will not be found in downloading our intelligence into robots, in extending our lives through nanotechnology, or in reducing our concepts of self to the level of computational machines. The answer lies in honoring the awesome, divine forces that flow through the universe— through our bodies, hearts, and minds, and through the digital world we call cyberspace.

Cyberspace has vast, untapped potential as a creative medium infused with divine presence. In this sense, as Kasparov glimpsed, cyberspace transcends its mathematical foundation of bits and bytes, 0s and 1s. At the same time, the fact that it contains some measure of divine creativity does not mean that when we enter it, we will magically develop spiritual sensitivity or awareness. Cyberspace is not a magic route to God. Spiritual evolution is always a personal choice. We have to do the work, and excruciatingly difficult work it is. In this sense, cyberspace may be less than we hope. If we wait passively for it to transform us into more conscious beings, our wait will be in vain. The job of spiritual growth is ours to do.

The enormous task of finding the spiritual in cyberspace must be performed in small, careful steps. For each voyager, the steps will be different. I have chosen as my first step to articulate a theology that embraces the powerful phenomenon of cyberspace. This theology seeks to answer the central question of how to include computers in our sacred lives. From this stance, I believe, we can reach into the future with hope. But this hope must be grounded in self-knowledge, ethically guided behavior, and clear communication with the sacred aspects of ourselves. If we achieve some small measure of these goals, then there is reason to hope that we will do our best to guide the ongoing evolution of the universe toward deeper spiritual awareness and action.

(1)

SPIRIT EVOLVING

In a complex of long, low buildings in the heart of Silicon Valley, Ranjit Makkuni was pushing the envelope of technology. A diminutive Hindu scientist at Xerox PARC in Palo Alto, Makkuni had been working hard for several years to perfect a state-of-the-art video conferencing system. This project had all the bells and whistles that time and money could supply—excellent video, fantastic sound reproduction, multiple screens and cameras. Makkuni had wired a room at Xerox PARC to a room in Portland and the results were impressive. Sitting in Palo Alto, one could viscerally feel another person's full presence, read his body language, and hear the subtle intonations of his speech, even though he was located hundreds of miles away. It was pretty close to real. But when Makkuni was asked, "Does this thing work?" he answered, "Oh, no." What was missing? He answered without missing a beat, "The prana."[1]

---

1. I am indebted to John Perry Barlow for this fine story.

Computers and the world they spawn, cyberspace, offer a wholly new field of experience. In light of this, Makkuni may be aiming for the wrong goal. A silicon-based domain may never transmit prana in the same way as carbon-based life forms do. This resolutely does not mean, however, that cyberspace is incapable of participating in the larger stream of sacred energy that we variously call God, Allah, Brahma, chi, or Tao. Even in their nascent and rudimentary form, computers are carving a new pathway into the divine force of the universe. If we move down this pathway as attentive and respectful explorers, we may find signs that computers exist on the same sacred continuum that we inhabit.

A sacred perspective broad enough to embrace the phenomenon of computers is not easy or self-evident. The idea that computers can include even a grain of sacred energy destabilizes our sense of self and our place in the world. Working through a comprehensive theological structure large enough to embrace the phenomenon of computation challenges us in the most surprising and unforeseen of ways. In fact, the daunting task of incorporating computers into our sacred understanding of the world represents our most potent personal and cultural challenge. At the same time, this odd interface offers enormous potential for deep growth and genuine empowerment.

Computers have become part of the very fabric of creation. Even now, those who never touch a computer personally—who don't use an ATM card or own a PC—are nonetheless surrounded by computer technology. Every time we pick up a phone, turn on the radio or television, get in our cars, climb on a bus, or go to the corner market for food, we participate in a world that is undergirded by a vast computerized system. The various types of computer systems that make up our world—from transportation to marketing to banking to communications—actually do the job they were designed to do remarkably well.

They work. As a result, they are growing and becoming more powerful with each day. Experts project that a billion people will be on-line by the turn of the millennium.

Computers are spawning a genuine revolution in human culture. As with any revolution, the long-term cultural and ethical ramifications remain unclear. We have no definitive sense of where we are going; we know simply that we are going there quickly. The sheer pace of change often keeps us from digging below the surface and developing the resources we need to make sense of computers on any deep, personal level. The most common response to the rapid change and uncertainty that computation has engendered is to fall on one side of an extreme— either elevate computers to the role of saviors or become neo-Luddites and cite them as the main source of our contemporary woes. In light of the ways in which computers are saturating our reality, these views are naive, maybe even dangerous.

When we refuse to incorporate computers into a coherent, comprehensive worldview that includes who we are materially, intellectually, emotionally, and spiritually, we perpetuate a host of time-honored Western dualisms between self and other, mind and body, nature and culture. These false dualisms—which have been the intellectual vogue for four hundred years—have created enormously damaging personal and environmental consequences. We live in a vast chasm of our own creation, located between the organic and the made, the sacred and the profane. When all around us is split into pieces, there is no center that holds. We are aliens in the very world we have constructed.

To repair this rift, we must begin with a fresh view. Each successive age throws forth a powerful new technology destined to change the world. From the first ax up through the wheel, the sextant, the clock, and the steam engine, the technologies that humans create fundamentally alter who we are. As each subsequent technology appears, it spawns a new element of cultural and personal understanding. If we look back through human history, we will see that every age has looked to its most powerful technology as a way of modeling the universe.

This enormously complex cultural evolution is not caused by technology in any simple sense. To conclude this would be to vastly oversimplify the dense interactions between individuals and culture, human creativity and the marks it leaves. It may be more appropriate to view the relationship between humans and their tools as a complex dance of becoming. We shape our tools and they in turn shape us. This process, which has been termed "coevolutionary" by some, is manifesting today in our relationship with computer technology. We create our tools. These tools in turn ask us to rethink our world, to expand our horizons and enlarge our wisdom. Ideally, we then bring this enlarged wisdom back to the tools and guide them to their next stage of development.

Our coevolutionary dance with computers affects us on many levels. Most obvious are the ways in which computer technology has altered the content of our material world. Computers have accelerated the process of mechanization begun in the age of industrialization. These sophisticated systems greatly enhance the fundamental power of the machine, further reducing the demands that daily living makes on our physical bodies. In addition, computers obviate the need for direct physical presence in many of our interactions. In today's computerized world, our bodies are coming to play a radically different role, both personally and socially. This dynamic further alters the relationship between our selves and the physical world we inhabit.

On an emotional and psychological level, computer technology is actively shifting our understanding of who we are, what forms our connections to one another take, and where we derive our sense of psychological health. Sherry Turkle, author of *Life on the Screen,* argues that the computer acts as a mirror reflecting a changing understanding of psychological health. She observes that one of the most significant features of our current computer-mediated environments is their relative anonymity. When bodies are absented from the interaction, people are free to choose any identity they wish. Men become women, women become men, shy people become bold, and bold people can try on a shy persona. In the world of computers, people can shape-shift at will, skimming through a revolving panorama of personae. Expressing multiple aspects of ourselves is becoming fashionable, but the jury is still out on whether this is a healthy development.

The life of the mind is also transforming rapidly as we find ourselves thinking through problems and solutions in terms of the paradigm of computation. We now inhabit a world that many of our greatest thinkers tell us is fundamentally computable. This basic idea finds its way into popular culture in a myriad of ways. For example, it is now commonly accepted that who we are can, in many ways if not most, be reduced to our DNA. What is DNA other than a string of computable numbers, one of nature's most fundamental algorithms? When we crack the code for DNA, the argument runs, we will be able to unlock the secrets of the universe—cure disease, reverse the aging process, achieve complete mastery over nature. In a similar vein, some of the brightest minds in physics today argue that the physical laws of the universe are algorithms. These ideas, and many others, suggest that the universe itself is nothing more than a giant computer.

These developments, applied individually, paint a deeply nihilistic picture. Computers are leading us away from our bodies and an integrated knowledge of self and toward a sterile, computable universe that can be reduced to bits and bytes, 0s and 1s. This view, while based on some very real truths, is ultimately not enough. Cyberspace does remove us from the physical, it does affect our social relationships, and algorithms can be found within the laws of the universe. But these statements do not constitute the entire truth of our complex and multi-faceted reality. A whole understanding of the world in which we find ourselves necessarily includes the physical, the emotional, the intellectual, and the spiritual. It is this latter piece that has been so markedly absent in our newly emerging understanding of the deeper implications of computation.

It would be foolish to assume that the life of the spirit is exempt from the slow but sure evolution we are undergoing. But the potential spiritual evolution inherent in cyberspace is subtle and difficult to grasp. What is easy to see is that we are living in a period of deep spiritual dislocation. Up to 30 percent of Americans will shift religious affiliations in their lifetime.[2] This is a significant movement that reflects a cultural sense of spiritual displacement. We are a people longing for sacred meaning. This longing will go unmet if it does not take into account the larger world in which we find ourselves. Today, the search for sacred meaning requires grappling with the powerful and radically new world of experience offered by computer technology.

To rediscover the sense of belonging and purpose that we thirst for requires that we approach the most powerful technology on our planet today with what is known in the Zen tradition as "beginner's mind." We must throw out our preconceived notions about what we believe computers are. We must enter a process of discovery that allows us to incorporate this remarkable phenomenon into a complete worldview, one coherent both with the world around us and with our intellectual, emotional, and spiritual connections to it. This does not mean that our earlier insights about the universe were wrong, merely that they may not be wholly adequate now. The computers we have created are mov-

---

2. Stephen J. Dubner, "Choosing My Religion," *New York Times Magazine,* March 31, 1996.

ing us forward on our evolutionary path. It is our responsibility to move our sacred understanding along with us.

Through a deepened, conscious relationship with computers, we have the potential to gain powerful insight into our evolutionary process. We may well find that computers reveal to us new understandings of our intellectual, emotional, cultural, and spiritual complexity. We must take care, however, not to conclude that these new understandings are now *the* new truth. Fresh insights must be synthesized into the larger sacred history of which they are a part.

The theology outlined in this book is another step along this ancient and future trajectory. It is an attempt to articulate how computer technology is revealing a novel understanding of divinity. This understanding is not an end in itself; rather, it is another beginning in our attempt to find rich meaning in ourselves and in the cosmos we inhabit. In the end, this may be the greatest power of the human urge for religious and theological insight—it is a line of questioning that has no concrete answers, contains multiple paradoxes, and has no closure. Theology is the process of plumbing our depths, discovering our humility and abilities in the face of awesome mysteries that we can only begin to approximate. If we can include computers in this process, we and they will only be the richer for it.

WHENCE WE HAVE COME

When Madonna's heavily mixed, techno-enhanced voice came trilling into our lives in the mid-1980s announcing that she was a "material girl" who lived in a "material world," she put her polished fingernail right on the pulse of our culture. Her reward? Instant stardom and riches almost beyond imagining.

Western culture at the brink of the millennium, in spite of the much-heralded entry into postmodernism, retains a fundamentally material perspective. Our world is heavily informed by the philosophies of modernism, a period that began roughly four hundred years ago and led us through the Industrial Revolution up to where we stand today, at the beginning of the so-called Information Age.

Modernism's rich and complex legacy gave birth to modern science. In doing so, it enabled Western culture to shed many of the simple and superstitious beliefs that previously held people in thrall to powerful monarchies and religious organizations. With modernity, we entered a period of self-discovery, of embracing our individuality, our intellect, and our ability to decipher the world around us. Unfortunately, something powerful was lost in this process as something new was gained.

With the rise of modern science, our sacred understanding of the world changed dramatically. Prior to the modernist period, in medieval times, people embraced a wholly different understanding of the divine. Those who lived in the Middle Ages believed that redemption was the primary goal of a spiritual life. The path to redemption focused on moving through what was often an exceedingly dismal life on earth with the hope of joining the heavenly father in Jerusalem on high after death. Religious teachings of the day emphasized beatific visions and direct experiences of the divine as signals or signposts along the way. In this context, the primary spiritual metaphor, as Paul Santmire points out in his book *The Travail of Nature,* was ascent—in essence, leaving this life to join the transcendent Father.

The metaphor of ascent was hardly new to the Judeo-Christian tradition of the Middle Ages. In fact, this metaphor can be traced back to the earliest roots of the Hebrew religion—for example, when Moses ascended the mountain to receive the Ten Commandments. This metaphor continued in the syncretic Christian tradition as the influence of the Greeks, Plotinus in particular, and the Gnostics was integrated into early Christianity. What is significant about the ancient metaphor of ascent in the Middle Ages was that even though the goal was to move up and away from the earth, the earth itself, the material world, was still considered infused with divinity. St. Francis of Assisi and St. Bonaventure, two of Christianity's most fervent devotees of the natural world, were active in this time period. Medieval thinkers commonly believed that God could be found as readily in the "book of nature" as in the Bible itself. This meant that the people of the Middle Ages essentially inhabited a sacred cosmos, one where God naturally infused all of creation.

By the early 1500s, Martin Luther (1483–1546), followed quickly by John Calvin (1509–1564), began the Protestant Reformation—a movement that would lay the groundwork for the modernist vision of a secularized, mechanical nature split off from a transcendent Father God ruling from on high. Luther and Calvin were products of their times, and neither man fully abandoned the traditions he had inherited from his medieval predecessors. Both theologians had the same primary concern—human salvation. Their unique contribution was to turn the metaphor of ascent on its head.

For these inaugural spokesmen of Protestantism, human salvation was achieved through the gracious descent of God into sinful humanity. The primary focus of the Reformation theologies shifted the sacred experience out of the general field of God and nature to a potentized, highly concentrated relationship between God and humanity. This is not to say that there is not ample evidence in the work of both Luther and Calvin of a vision of sacred nature. In fact, both men embraced nature as a natural extension of God and a locus for God's expression. The important shift was toward a God who was so all-powerful, so willful, and so in control of each and every aspect of existence that humans could never elect to ascend to meet this divine presence. For Luther and Calvin, ascent simply ascribed too much power to humanity. As Santmire points out, Calvin took this inverted metaphor and shaped it into a powerful imperative for humans to carry out God's will through entering the stream of history and altering it to meet the divine plan. This vocational doctrine would become highly influential in the centuries to come.

For the people of the medieval period, as for the Reformers, the God/human relationship had three primary aspects.[3] The first was that the world was created by a personal God. Therefore, qualities that humans could embody—such as love, devotion, and judgment—were viewed as primordial and eternal. Second, humans were believed to have been created in the image of God and were therefore privileged as the "crown of creation." Third, life on earth was seen as only the beginning of our eternal existence. After one passed from the earth, he or she would ultimately experience the eternal pleasures of heaven or the eternal tortures of hell. When the founding fathers of the modern era, the great Enlightenment thinkers, Galileo (1564–1642), Descartes (1596–1650), and Newton (1642–1727), came on the scene, they inherited these basic Christian suppositions.

In one of the subtle ironies of the modern period, these early and enormously influential scientists were inspired to formulate their mechanistic visions of the world in order to protect their theological beliefs. Luther and Calvin's emphasis on a transcendent, omnipotent God freed people to reimagine the natural world as devoid of any power of its own. Without God's descent, the material world was essentially dead. Matter was alive only when God chose to enter it. This belief was crystallized in the pivotal year 1543 with the publication of two treatises

---

3. See David Ray Griffin, *God & Religion in the Postmodern World,* chapter 1.

that would alter the course of Western history. That was the year Vesalius published his famous examination of the human body, a work derived from his years of dissecting human corpses. Dissection, as a scientific exploration, would have been unthinkable for the people of the Middle Ages, who believed that the corpse was a sacred entity. That same year, Copernicus shattered the belief that the earth was the center of the universe, further displacing the notion of divine centrality in the material world.

The seeds of a radically dualist world were sown with God on high and a dead world below. In order to protect the transcendent Creator, Galileo, Newton, and Descartes would carefully shepherd these seeds into fully blown visions of a mechanistic world ruled by a fully transcendent God. Newton reimagined the world as a giant machine, set in motion by God. Soon, the machine itself became the focus and scientists of the day concentrated on mapping its pieces. As the story the scientists told about the world became more fully rendered, the need to include the divine spark became less and less intelligible. Soon, Western thinkers came to believe that the laws of science could adequately explain the machine itself. God had become unnecessary.

In the modern era, the mechanistic world of matter claimed the superior role in human understanding. Historian Edwin Burtt has described the unfolding of modernism as follows:

The gloriously romantic universe of Dante and Milton, that set no bounds to the imagination of man as it played over space and time, had now been swept away. Space was identified with the realm of geometry, time with the continuity of number. The world that people had thought themselves living in—a world rich with color and sound, redolent with fragrance, filled with gladness, love and beauty, speaking everywhere of purposive harmony and creative ideals—was crowded into minute concerns in the brains of scattered organic beings. The really important world outside was hard, cold, colorless, silent, and dead; a world of quantity, a world of mathematically computable motions in mechanical regularity. The world of qualities as immediately perceived by man became just a curious and quite minor effect of that infinite machine beyond.[4]

The outcome of the modernist trajectory for our sacred understanding was either scientific atheism, embraced by many, or a highly spiritualized experience of the divine that had little connection to the world. For the most influential thinkers of the Enlightenment, the latter was the preferred solution. Descartes, Newton, Kant, and Darwin all retained a sacred understanding; it was simply split off from the material basis of reality. Later Protestant thinkers cooperated with this new vision by promoting the idea that the only correct way to reach God was to transcend the natural world. Nature had become secularized and our relation to it had become instrumental.

The last two hundred years of the modern era have been characterized as the Industrial Age. During this time, progress has been the clarion call of Western culture. As science claimed the keys to the natural world, busily creating theories, concepts, and hypotheses to map it, our sense of control over the world increased enormously. We began the process of building machines that could utilize the resources of dead nature far more efficiently than brute human strength ever could. We observed the fruits of a rational industrial world—increased food supply, cleaner living conditions, lower mortality rates—and rejoiced in our power. All in all, progress appeared to be a superior path.

---

4. Quoted in H. Paul Santmire, *The Travail of Nature,* page 134.

Within a few hundred years, we had become devout materialists. We found ourselves living in a world of objects we felt we could control. This new outlook was buttressed by the Protestant theologies of the day. Protestantism had developed a strong work ethic that claimed that the good Christian life was characterized by diligent hard work and strict piety. This ethic encouraged people to acquire and save increasing amounts of material wealth, which soon became the outward sign of the good Protestant. In Europe and America, the devout rapidly accumulated vast reserves of money, a trend that was not only socially sanctioned but theologically encouraged. This accumulation, as the now-classic works of Max Weber and R. H. Tawney point out, provided the seeds of capitalism.

The metaphor of God the great clockmaker descending to animate the world had transmuted into an ideology of progress and dominion over nature. Autonomy and scientific understanding conferred enormous power on humanity, elevating the values of rationality and correct social behavior as the highest goods. The scientific society that these trends produced left little room for a faith fully integrated into the worlds of the organic and the made. Freed from the moorings of our religious symbols and norms, we became like the universe we modeled—autonomous individuals moving through a valueless world.

FROM PROGRESS TO PROCESS

Fifty years ago, the first modern computer was built. Named ENIAC, for the Electronic Numerical Integrator and Computer, this machine required its own refrigerated room at IBM, complete with a large staff of attendants. The powers of ENIAC would seem laughable to anyone with a five-dollar calculator today. Nevertheless, with this unwieldy machine, the age on whose cusp we now stand was launched.

Computer technology forms the basis of the much-heralded Information Age. This age differs from the age of industry in one absolutely fundamental way. The center of gravity of the Information Age is not matter, but information and knowledge. According to *A Magna Carta for the Knowledge Age,* coauthored by Esther Dyson, George Gilder, George Keyworth, and Alvin Toffler, the "central event of the 20th century is the overthrow of matter."[5] This rather dramatic statement goes right to the heart of the issue. We are entering a time when the truths of modernism—that the world is made up of discrete, material objects that can be physically mapped, described, and, in theory, controlled—are being replaced by a new set of understandings based on the primacy of nonmaterial events, or packets of information, that are dynamically linked in a vast, invisible terrain known as cyberspace.

William Gibson, the writer who coined the word *cyberspace* in his now-classic science fiction novel *Neuromancer,* claims that the term was meant to suggest "the point at which the media flow together and surround us. It's the ultimate extension of the exclusion of daily life. With cyberspace as I describe it you can literally wrap yourself in media and not have to see what's really going on around you." The authors of *A Magna Carta for the Knowledge Age* cast cyberspace in another light when they write, "More ecosystem than machine, cyberspace is a bio-electronic environment that is literally universal: It exists every-

---

5. Esther Dyson, George Gilder, George Keyworth, and Alvin Toffler, *Cyberspace and the American Dream: A Magna Carta for the Knowledge Age,* release 1.2, updated January 11, 1995, available at: http://www.pff.org

where there are telephone wires, coaxial cables, fiber-optic lines or electromagnetic waves."[6]

A vast, pulsing, electronic world, cyberspace encircles the globe. When we enter it, we go into a place that feels removed from the physical world. It is a space composed of information, images, and symbols. In many ways, this world of pure images is the crowning achievement of a Western trajectory of thought that began with Plato in his apocryphal cave. Plato argued that we are trapped in the cave of matter and can see the real world of intellectual ideas only as the shadows these ideas cast upon the walls of the cave. Plato's call was for us to emerge from the cave and live fully within the world of ideal forms, the life of the mind. Cyberspace can be interpreted as the Platonic realm incarnate.[7]

The mathematical basis of cyberspace furthers its relationship to this Platonic ideal. The software that forms the technical heart of cyberspace, the instructions that make it run, are all coded in binary sequences of either 0s or 1s, bits and bytes, or, to put it more simply, as electricity "on" or electricity "off." These glorified calculators use mathematics to create a palpable world of experience analogous to Plato's world of forms.

The notion of a mathematically based reality can be traced to Pythagoras. For Pythagoras, as for Plato, the real basis of the material world was located in intellectual ideas, or pure forms, that could be seen only by the mind's eye. Mathematics was the best representation of the ordered intellect. As such, it was viewed as a powerful, sacred language that could reveal the true nature of the universe. These quasi-mystical beliefs were later adopted by modern science, when it declared

6. Ibid., page 2.
7. See, in particular, Michael Heim, *The Metaphysics of Virtual Reality.*

mathematics as the foundational principle of its effort to discover the natural laws of the universe.

Scientific thought holds that all physical reality, as well as the laws that govern it, are made comprehensible through mathematical calculation. This belief has created a privileged role for mathematics in the world of science. In fact, there is a tacit understanding among scientists that the more mathematics is involved in a certain area of exploration, the more legitimate and pure the outcomes of that exploration will be. In this context, physics—which is almost purely mathematical—has long been viewed as the ultimate scientific discipline.

In today's rarefied realm of higher mathematics and physics, scientists continue to pursue formulae that describe the laws governing the universe. Recent examples of such attempts are chaos theory and superstring theory. These mathematical systems are rooted in the belief that the world can be described through the abstract set of symbols that we call numbers. Many physicists see themselves as modern-day Platonic explorers, using math to uncover that which already exists. Roger Penrose, the British mathematician, explicated this view when he claimed that "there is a sort of 'Platonic' realm quite separate from the physical realm, where there exist objects such as the Mandelbrot set. These objects are not invented by mathematicians, they are discovered."

In the same vein, a number of people in the world of computer technology believe that cyberspace is a distinct and separate Platonic reality that we are only now coming to discover. Some take the idea even further. For those who believe that abstract mathematics constitutes the truest description of reality, the physical world is the simulation and the world of cyberspace is the more fundamental reality. The computer, in this view, is the tool that we use to access this preexisting reality. Benjamin Woolley, in his book *Virtual Worlds*, summarizes this belief when he writes, "Maybe the universe is not so much a book as a computer, everything that exists within it the product of some algorithm. If so, this would mean that [the computer] would truly be universal: given the right table of behavior, and sufficient time, it could reproduce an entire virtual universe."[8]

It is seductive to view cyberspace as no more than a continuation of the modernist, scientific worldview, supported by an even more ancient Platonic bias toward the nonphysical world. But cyberspace is more complex than that. A bioelectronic ecosystem linked into the physical ecosystem, cyberspace reveals the inadequacy of the modern vision of discrete, autonomous individuals cohabiting in a world of simple cause and effect. In cyberspace, all is connected, all is relational and relative. For example, when one surfs the World Wide Web, one does not travel in a hierarchical, linear fashion. One moves through the Web on an almost infinite variety of pathways that are related and connected by virtue of their participation in the network of cyberspace. As we move through this computational space, our fundamental notions about the world are challenged, and even Plato's classical image only partially satisfies our desire to understand.

To further complicate the story, cyberspace is also a world of experience. For the first time in history, we can enter with others what appears an abstract domain and populate it with human experiences. We are creating a communal realm of knowledge and information that can be shared. This is a profound realization. In one of the great ironies of our time, modern science has spawned an invention that enables us to begin with an abstractly defined world and derive from it a new phenomenology that ultimately challenges the very presuppositions of the world that gave it birth in the first place. In other words, computation may ultimately challenge the hegemony of the scientific, material worldview.

---

8. Benjamin Woolley, *Virtual Worlds,* page 70.

THE DiVinE PROCESS

In the earliest weeks of writing this book, I had an experience that I view in retrospect as a gift of grace. I was transcribing into my computer an interview I had conducted with a theologian. This interview had taken place in an Indian restaurant in a small shopping mall in Southern California. Throughout our discussion, soft Indian music was playing in the background. At the time, I was only marginally aware of the music, but as I began to transcribe, I noticed quite clearly what a lovely environment the gentle tones created. Toward the end of the interview, I heard myself saying, "And we have to acknowledge that the sacred is present in computers. Once we acknowledge that, then we have a basis for making ethical and moral decisions about them. . . ." As I typed these words into my computer, I was suddenly suffused with a palpable experience of divine presence connecting myself and the digital world into which I was feeding my words. For the first time, I viscerally felt the connection that I had stubbornly believed for so many years must be present.

I arrived at this luminous moment through a long and circuitous path. Over the years, I have tenaciously held on to a deep intuition that whispered that if the world is sacred, then there must be a sacred aspect to each and every piece of it. Fleshing out this intuition into a set of specific qualities that can be found in computer technology has been a painstaking process. To touch the palpable presence of divinity at that juncture in the world was a gift beyond measure.

A sacred understanding of cyberspace requires a reconciliation between scientific and religious worldviews, perspectives that in the wake of modernism have inhabited diametrically opposed corners of our reality. Science claims the seemingly incontrovertible ground of logical, rational inquiry. It arrives at an understanding of the world through proven, quantifiable analysis. Though its truths are funneled through the experiences of humans, science seeks to avoid subjective human experience through proven methodologies. Primary among these is the requirement that experimental data be repeatable in different settings by different people over time. Science focuses on the objective and the tangible, achieving its goals by dividing the world into smaller and smaller pieces.

Religion locates its power specifically in the realm of subjective human experience. Although spiritual calling is a deeply personal matter, religions the world over have developed complex rules for human conduct and sophisticated methods for achieving spiritual progress that constitute a specific methodology. Even so, the focus of religion and spiritual discipline has been on the subjective sacred connections between all that is. *Re-ligio* in Latin means "to connect." Theology is an attempt to articulate the nature of these connections from the perspective of the subjective and the ineffable.

A theology of cyberspace begins with the attempt to merge the worlds of the objective and the subjective, the tangible and the intangible. It asks that we expand our notion of spirituality to include the machine, traditionally the stronghold of science. And it asks us to expand our understanding of science to include the notion of an ineffable force of connection working in the realm of the tangible and the objective. In seeking to build a bridge between these divergent worlds, the single most important concept we can turn to is evolutionary process.

When Charles Darwin set out on the *Beagle,* he was a committed deist. This means that he believed there existed a grand design in nature and that the blueprints for that design were drafted and executed by God. From that point forward, however, God steps aside. Much to Darwin's dismay, the evidence he accumulated while on his journeys pointed to a very different truth. The world that he found was in no way complete; instead, it was in the process of ongoing change and evolution. This discovery caused Darwin to undergo a lifelong search for a way to reconcile his data with his God. He would remain frustrated in this attempt until his death. In 1860 and 1861, Darwin related his confusion to Harvard botanist Asa Gray in a series of letters. In one, he wrote, "I cannot think that the world . . . is the result of chance; and yet I cannot look at each separate thing as the result of Design. . . . I am, and shall ever remain, in a hopeless muddle."[9]

The heart of the difficulty for Darwin lay in the concept of chance. Evolution depends intimately on the idea that chance mutations occur during the process of reproduction. In most cases, these mutations are not beneficial to the organism. However, in a few cases, they will prove superior and will offer the organism a competitive advantage according to the environment in which it finds itself. What is important to note here is that the two events—the mutation and the advantage it confers—are separate yet interdependent events. Mutations occur randomly. Those that will be selected as beneficial depend on the organism's interaction with its environment. There is no grand designer conducting either the selection or its subsequent effects.

This particular understanding of chance blasted a permanent hole in the idea of a fully determined universe. As Darwin reluctantly proved, chance and random occurrences are integral to the process of evolution. This idea would prove foundational for his intellectual descendants. For Jacques Monod, the great French biologist, chance and chance alone is the motor of evolution. For neo-Darwinists, such as Stephen Jay Gould, evolution is the process of change, moving

---

9. As quoted in Charles Birch, *A Purpose for Everything*, page 39.

nowhere in particular, fueled by chance mutations at the genetic level. Even more renegade theories such as those proposed by the Russian biologist Kropotkin, who argued that the motor of change is actually cooperation, not competition, held on to the notion of chance as primary to the process. As biologist Lewis Thomas wrote, "The capacity to blunder slightly is the real marvel of DNA. Without this special attribute, we would still be anaerobic bacteria."[10]

The overthrow of a deterministic universe ruled by a deterministic God from on high opened the way for a very different understanding of divinity. Though most biologists following Monod and the neo-Darwinian school would deny it, chance leaves open the possibility of purpose in the universe.[11] Darwin hinted at this when he wrote to Asa Gray, "I cannot persuade myself that a beneficent and omnipotent God would have designedly created the Ichneumonidae with the express intention of feeding within the living bodies of Caterpillars, or that a cat should play with mice. Not believing this, I see no necessity in the belief that the eye was expressly designed. On the other hand, I cannot anyhow be contented to view this wonderful universe, and especially the nature of man, and to conclude that everything is the result of brute force. I am inclined to look at everything as resulting from designed laws, with the details, whether good or bad, left to the working out of what we may call chance. Not that this notion at all satisfies me. . . . But the more I think the more bewildered I become."[12]

What Darwin failed to recognize was that chance's two evolutionary bedfellows—self-organization and self-transcendence—carve a pathway directly toward the divine principle in the universe. Chance

---

10. Ibid., page 35.

11. See Charles Birch, *A Purpose for Everything*.

12. Ibid., page 40.

does not work solely by itself.[13] When contextualized into the environment in which evolution occurs, chance can only be understood as one aspect of the larger process of evolutionary change. Every organism lives within the context of its environment. When a mutation occurs, the organism takes this new feature and adapts itself to its environment. This adaptive step implies some level of self-determination and freedom in the process that transcends the mechanism of pure chance. Viewed from the macro level, chance does indeed form a basic motor of evolution, as scientific evidence has amply demonstrated. But from a meta-perspective, evolution is more than random mutation. Evolution continually seeks to transcend what it has given birth to. It achieves this self-transcendence through a self-organizational process of incorporating change. In simplified terms, a mutation occurs (chance), the organism responds to its environment in terms of the change (self-organization), and if the mutation is beneficial, a new level of evolution is reached (self-transcendence).

The concepts of self-organization and self-transcendence add a radically other dimension to the scientific understanding of evolution. It is the self-transcending aspect of evolution that makes sense of the continual emergence of new possibilities in the universe. Self-transcendence is fundamentally creative. Creativity works together with chance to produce increasing complexity and organization in the world. This movement toward increasing organization forms the fundamental direction of evolution, and it reveals a deeper purpose lurking in its depths. Evolution continually brings new possibilities into manifestation, possibilities that are increasingly complex and ordered. From a

---

13. For a much more in-depth look at this issue, see Christian de Duve, *Vital Dust,* and Charles Birch, *A Purpose for Everything.*

theological perspective, this evolutionary purpose forms the very heart of divine manifestation in the world.

The idea of evolution having a larger spiritual purpose was very much in the air when Darwin began his scientific explorations. It was amply evident to some of the pre-Darwinian philosophers that evolution contained a deep purpose beyond random change. This purpose was characterized as a movement toward richer and deeper creative diversification and complexity. Darwin was so wedded to the idea of a wholly deterministic God that he was blinded to the glimmers of theological purpose in his own discoveries. The idea that there could be a divine force that necessarily coexisted with random chance simply escaped him.

Philosopher Ken Wilber traces the spiritualized idea of evolution back to the work of Friedrich Schelling (1775–1854), a German philosopher who wrote almost six decades before Darwin published his work on biological evolution. Schelling maintained that the basic drive of evolution was God. God manifested within the process of evolution in the form of self-organization and self-transcendence. Along with Hegel, Schelling argued that through these forces, the divine permeates the whole evolutionary process. Evolution is the movement of the divine toward the divine, a bidirectional flow of the inherent spirit in matter moving up to meet transcendent spirit and of transcendent spirit moving down to meet spirit in matter. At every level in the evolutionary hierarchy, the divine manifests as the creative aspect of the process. Wilber writes, "This is a truly stunning vision . . . of Spirit descending into even the lowest state and ascending back to itself, with Spirit nonetheless *fully present at each and every stage* as the *process* of its own self-realization and self-actualization, its own self-unfolding and self-enfolding development, a divine play of Spirit present in every single movement of the Kosmos, yet finding more and more of itself as its own play proceeds, dancing fully and divine in every gesture of the universe, never really lost and never really found, but present from the start and all along, a wink and a nod from the radiant Abyss."[14]

Spirit is by definition the force that connects. Therefore, spiritual purpose is revealed through the continuities that lie between the seemingly discrete aspects of the universe. Chance mutation at the genetic level is a discontinuous process. Mutations are, by definition, discrete and random. Causes, such as radiation, can be identified, but these too are discrete and discontinuous. No single cause or set of causes can be identified that sew together the whole evolutionary process. Evolution seen through the scientific lens of cause and effect leads to a discontinuous view of discrete particles interacting through chance. It should come as no surprise that if this is the only lens through which one views evolution, one will remain blind to the idea of a purposeful universe infused with spirit.

Divine essence, manifesting as creative self-transcendence, forms the continuity that ties the evolutionary process together. This divine, creative force permeates all of reality, from the atom to the human to the biosphere, binding it together into one continuous whole. This view does not deny that discontinuities exist. It simply says that there are also continuities, that the whole is related internally through the ineffable energy of the divine, as well as externally through discrete cause and effect.

Divine spirit forms the connective web that ties an organism to its environment. Through this connection an organism manifests creative novelty, self-organization, and self-transcendence. Conversely, when

---

14. Ken Wilber, *Sex, Ecology, Spirituality*, page 489. See pages 485–93 for a discussion of Schelling, Hegel, and evolution.

the environment in which an organism lives is dissected into discrete units, it loses its sacred meaning. For example, even though a human is made up of atoms, molecules, and cells, one cannot define the totality of a person solely on the basis of his or her atomic structure. One cannot adequately define even a cell based on its atomic structure. A complete understanding of any entity must take place from the perspective of the whole. This perspective requires an understanding of connection, of continuity, as well as discontinuity.

If divinity is central to the evolutionary process, it then follows that spirit and matter could have coexisted since the inception of the universe. The Jesuit paleontologist Teilhard de Chardin voiced this perspective when he wrote in *The Divine Milieu*, "Every genesis, or evolution, presupposes interconnections, mutual or reciprocal dependence, with no breach. It implies in the being that is forming itself a kinship between the composing elements; thus a static cosmos, fragmented in make-up, is unthinkable. If everything forms itself, everything must hold together. Matter and spirit, then, as we know them in our universe, are not two separate substances, set side by side and differing in nature. They are two distinct aspects of one single cosmic stuff."[15] That single cosmic stuff is the creative process of spirit in action in the world.

Evolution is the movement of matter reaching toward spirit. Involution, on the other hand, is the process of spirit coming down into matter. As the universe evolves and becomes more complex, it exhibits increasing levels of creative change. This in turn makes more room for the transcendent nature of the divine to enter the world. From the perspective of creative transformation, from a God's-eye view, these two processes are one and the same. The overall purpose of evolution and

---

15. Pierre Teilhard de Chardin, *The Divine Milieu*, pages 21–22.

involution is identical—to make room for greater levels of rich, creative experience, for the actualization of spirit in the world.

This view points to a wholly new understanding of divinity. The divine as creativity in process does not rule from on high, determining all outcomes. This divinity empowers the creatures of the universe through its own creative nature. It connects all that is through the continual process of creative transcendence and evolution. Perhaps most important, it leaves room for the mechanistic understandings of science to join hands with a spiritual perspective that assumes the evolution of consciousness, soul, and spirit as integral to the development of the universe.

As the divine force moves into the world through the pathway of evolution, it manifests increasing levels of spiritual consciousness on the material plane. This seemingly random process has created an extraordinary achievement. It has produced a species capable not only of consciousness but of reflective self-consciousness. As Teilhard de Chardin argued, this represents a new stage in evolution, one marked by the capacity for deep spiritual and intellectual experience. Ken Wilber, summarizing Hegel and Schelling, echoes this idea when he writes, "Spirit *knows itself objectively* as Nature; *knows itself subjectively* as Mind; and knows itself absolutely as Spirit—the Source, the Summit, and the Eros of the whole sequence."[16]

As self-conscious beings, we are now in the unique position of participating actively in the ongoing evolution of the planet. A fundamental piece of this evolutionary trajectory has to do with making conscious our role in the spiritual evolution of the universe. When we live in a world of discontinuities, a world divided, we perpetuate the most damaging aspects of modernism. Nature continues to be an object

---

16. Ken Wilber, *Sex, Ecology, Spirituality*, page 489.

to be defiled; we understand ourselves as radically individual, a stance that results in alienation, lack of community, and loneliness; we pursue superficial, materialistic goals, skimming along the surface of life. When we find ourselves in a world splintered, our deepest selves become splintered as well. The only way out of this state of personal, social, and environmental malaise is through an evolutionary process that incorporates spirit, connection, and wholeness.

In the ongoing process of spiritual evolution, cyberspace has a special role to play. When we begin to see evolution from a spiritual perspective as both a fundamental feature of the universe and the source of its essential sacred nature, a whole new vision of reality unfolds before us. In this vision, the spiritual basis of the universe is understood as creative events unfolding in time. Cyberspace reflects this basic, sacred truth as it creates a world of experience capable of enormous richness and diversity that is *derived from essentially nonphysical, creative events unfolding in time.* Cyberspace drives the first experiential wedge into the hegemony of the modernist perspective of quantifiable matter as the only genuine basis of reality. Cyberspace can help guide us toward a reconciliation of the major schisms of our time, those between science and spirit, between the organic world and the world that we create.

Cyberspace's web of dynamic, energetic connections is composed of information presented in such a way that we can experience it. We can send and receive e-mail, talk to people far away on the phone, watch televised images broadcast from afar in the comfort of our homes. In cyberspace, what is ephemeral has also become an essential feature of what we think of as real. But, one might counter, these experiences are not real in the same way as the telephone, the television set, or the person sitting next to me at the movies. They do not have a physical reality. But cyberspace, like the creative aspect of evolution, is woven into our physical reality. One cannot watch televised images without a television set any more than one can experience the presence of the sacred without the benefit of a physical body. The events that comprise cyberspace are an aspect of the larger force of the divine that manifests in the physical world as creative process unfolding in time. Both depend on a complex mix of matter and experience to achieve manifestation.

The role of cyberspace in our evolution is intricate and can at times be troubling. Judging by the reaction in the popular media to computers and the people who develop them, we live in a culture that worships at the altar of technology. We attribute God-like qualities to computers, assuming them to be all-knowing and all-powerful. We feel diminished by their powers, frightened and out of control. We confer great honor and wealth on the priesthood that understands and uses them. This techno-worship verges on the ancient sin of idolatry. Instead of understanding that the divine infuses computers and weaving them into a larger web of sacred experience, we assume the power comes from the computer; we give credence to the creature rather than the creator.[17] This is a lazy response. When we refuse to acknowledge the sacred spectrum to which both computers and we belong, we stand in danger of further diminishing, rather than enriching, our spiritual lives.

Creative process forms the soul of cyberspace. The source of richness and potential in this vast, electronic web of experience is spirit. The divine expresses itself in the digital terrain through the vast, global communication networks that are now beginning to display rudimentary self-organizing properties. It expresses itself in the arcane realms of artificial evolution and artificial life, areas where self-transcendence and self-organization generated by the digital environment are every-

---

17. I am indebted to a conversation with Granville Henry for this distinction.

day facts. And it expresses itself in the continual, creative interactions that constitute the relationship between human culture and its digital tools.

If we can allow ourselves to understand the deeper, sacred mechanisms of cyberspace, we can begin to experience it as a medium of grace. Grace traditionally means an experience of divinity that reaches our conscious selves; we suddenly become aware of God working in our lives. Bringing the experience of creative process into our conscious lives offers the possibility that we can begin once again to experience the divine flowing through our reality. Once we have developed the sensitivity to understand, we find the world around us infused with sacred process. With this understanding, we can begin to embrace the wholeness of the world we call home in both its natural and technological aspects.

The evolution of spirit and the evolution of matter converge in an ongoing partnership of becoming. Each follows its own course, but the two must be considered together. The evolution of matter is the realm of science; much work has been done to understand its patterns. The evolution of spirit, however, is a more mysterious terrain. An exploration of the evolution of spirit forms the heart of this book. It is my primary contention that cyberspace has a fundamental role to play in the ongoing movement of soul and spirit through the universe. This is a many-leveled discussion that will take us from the heart of the digital terrain itself to the dynamic between cyberspace and the world of human agency. Throughout, the focus will be on the centrality of spiritual evolution to the health and healing of ourselves, our communities, and our world.

(2)

L I F E   D I V I N E

Every day for the last fifteen years, Ralph Abraham, a taut and wiry professor at UC Santa Cruz, has been logging on to the Internet. Of course, fifteen years ago, it wasn't called that. What we think of as the Internet today began its life as the National Science Foundation Network (NSFnet), a means for researchers to communicate quickly between laboratories. Abraham, a mathematician and one of the founding thinkers of chaos theory, recognized early on that this powerful communications medium was more than a research tool.

From his front-row seat, Abraham has made a hobby of tracking the complex evolution over the wires that we now call cyberspace. Abraham traces the earliest days of the Net to a time almost a hundred years ago. "We are really in the late phase of the telephone revolution," he claims. "The interconnection of everyone increased catastrophically in a very short time, starting around the turn of the century with the development of telephone wires. It's these same telephone wires today

46

that support the Internet and the World Wide Web. What we are really doing is working out the telephone system."

The telephone system today is rapidly moving into its next stage of evolution. To recall William Gibson's prophetic words, in cyberspace, all the media begin to flow together. The voice of the telephone is rapidly merging with textual, graphical, and video images. This rich terrain can be accessed through a variety of wired and wireless devices. In fact, the last part of this decade will most likely be marked by an explosion of choices in terms of access appliances. The World Wide Web, the multimedia element of the Internet, though still in its infancy, represents a crucial stage in this ongoing revolution.

Abraham is one of a handful of people who have traced the emergence of the Web back to its beginnings. In 1989, a young graduate student named Tim Burners-Lee came up with the idea for the Web and wrote the first browser. Then, in a completely unconnected step, Mark Andreesson, then a graduate student at the University of Illinois and now a multimillionaire founder of the publicly held company Netscape, wrote the second browser. Andreeson's browser added the functionality that the first browser lacked. Both of these events, which were unrelated, happened in research labs, not in the R&D departments of big computer companies. Neither of these necessary events was coordinated or logical. Both men were, according to Abraham, inspired.

"The WWW is miraculous," Abraham states categorically. "It is theological creativity in action. If you look at the Web, there are all these different pieces of software without which it couldn't run. These pieces were created by volunteers, people who were responding to a kind of divine guidance. They were being pushed toward creative synthesis. The miraculous way the parts go together can't be a coincidence. There were too many different inventions in totally different labs."

The emergent pattern that Abraham calls "theological creativity" is a recurrent theme in his work. Abraham's sunny office, located in a small complex of similar offices, literally hums. He has at least three large computer workstations running at all times. On the screens are displayed glorious fractal images, graphical renderings of complex chaotic equations. In the process of completing his latest book, Abraham has been exploring an arcane corner of chaos theory that has been previously overlooked. The mathematics he employs to create fractal images for his book are unlike any I have seen before. Rather than the familiar nautilus or fernlike patterns, Abraham's equations have generated topographies that appear more like mountain ranges or forests—complex, natural-looking images that retain the rough edges of things grown by nature.

The ecosystems that nature grows rarely reflect the purity and cleanness of the created world. There is an odd symmetry between natural ecosystems and cyberspace, a bioelectronic ecosystem that more closely resembles Abraham's fractals than it does the neat wiring diagrams of an engineer. Imagine for a moment a schematic of the nodes, wires, and wireless links that comprise cyberspace. We might begin by plotting the terrestrial network, a vast pulsing web of telephone wires and dedicated networks linked together. This net would crisscross the globe, appearing in some areas as almost impossibly dense, while in others it would be represented by only a few lines. To that network we would add the multitude of communications satellites that circumnavigate the earth. Each satellite would receive and bounce back millions of data links, both to the terrestrial network and to other wireless media. Now take this complex picture and put it in time. What would quickly emerge would appear like a time-lapsed photograph of a thickly tangled meadow in active growth. The image would display chaotic, seemingly random patterns of continual development. New nodes and connections would emerge moment by moment. The more connections added, the more growth the network would display, each node responsible for thousands of new connections.

When we attempt to understand the inner workings of the world of networked computing that we call the Internet, we find ourselves quickly coming face to face with a fundamental question: What is driving this phenomenal growth? Certainly, no one person or organization is in control. It is as if it has a life of its own, its growth following a quasi-organic pattern of evolutionary development. On closer inspection, we come to see that this pattern is fundamentally an emergent process, growing from the bottom up.

DiViNE BETWEEN THE LiNES

The global Net and its offspring, the World Wide Web, are classic examples of emergent entities. The Net meets the basic definition of emergence—its whole is greater than the sum of its parts. If one picks the Net apart into its constituent elements—silicon-based hardware, digitized information known as software, and electricity—one can understand the pieces that go into creating it. But from these pieces, one cannot predict the extraordinarily complex behavior that characterizes the global computer network. Just as one cannot look at an ant and extrapolate from it the complexity of an ant colony, one cannot arrive at the totality of the Net through an examination of hardware and software alone. Something else is active in the equation.

When one finds oneself in the presence of an exquisite piece of sculpture, such as a masterwork by Henry Moore or Alexander Calder, the form of the piece itself is what first draws one in. But as one spends more time with the work, one begins to notice that the spaces surrounding the piece are as much a part of its definition as the piece itself. In the world of art, this is called the "negative space," referring to the way in which the absence of material contributes to the aesthetic of the space in which tangible material exists.

This notion of the whole as dependent on both its positive and negative, or its tangible and intangible, elements is hardly new. Philosophical and scientific precedent can be found for this idea in traditions ranging from the ancient Chinese notion of yin and yang to the fundamentals of modern physics. The basic truth revealed here is that these two elements, positive and negative, require each other for completion. Negative cannot exist without positive any more than day can exist without night, emptiness without substance, good without evil. The same is true in cyberspace. In order to appreciate it fully, we must look closely at both the relationship between what we can positively apprehend and the spaces that surround these elements. The key to emergence in cyberspace lies in the area that we cannot readily see or touch. It exists in the space between the hardware and the software.

Cyberspace is not located in a piece of software sitting on a shelf, nor can it be found in a hunk of hardware with no software brains loaded into it. By definition, cyberspace is what happens when software and hardware are joined together and put *into motion*. Cyberspace is born from process. In cyberspace, just as in Newtonian space, this process is intangible. We cannot see it or touch it. We can, however, touch the products of the process. We can view the graphical and textual stuff that software and hardware generate. But, by the time the products of the process reach our conscious minds, the process itself is already complete. The moment of creation passes below the surface of our awareness and we are left with the objective entities it has given birth to. We are so accustomed to accepting the fruits of process as our primary reality that we overlook the moment where being and becoming are one and the same, the moment of creative action, of process itself. It is here, in the interaction between the hardware and the software, that the sacred locus of computation can be found.

In the world of computer science, software is defined as consisting of algorithms. An algorithm is simply a string of code, a mathematical equation that, in theory, creates a map for the computer to follow. For example, a computer algorithm can be an instruction for the computer to go to place X in the program each time it runs into string Y. In and of itself, this algorithm is nothing more than an abstraction, just as a mathematical equation is an abstraction. An algorithm has no concrete reality of its own. That is, until it is put into motion in the context of a computer.

When a set of algorithms that we call software runs in a computer, something remarkable begins to happen. The abstraction becomes a field of experience that we call cyberspace. It is in this moment that the emergent quality of cyberspace makes itself known. The essential motor of this process, the spiritual center of cyberspace, is the fundamental sacred force that infuses all reality: divine creativity in action. The emergent dynamic found between the hardware and software in cyberspace is an aspect of divinity itself. In other words, the cosmic force that drives the movement and unfolding of reality is the same force as that which drives the continual, moment-by-moment emergence of the world of cyberspace.

THE DiViNE PROCESS

To understand how novelty unfolds both in cyberspace and in the larger world to which it is intimately wedded, we turn our attention to a field of inquiry called process philosophy. Process philosophy offers a set of building blocks for conceptualizing those aspects of the world that we cannot necessarily see or touch but that nonetheless undergird all that is. From the perspective of process, the traditional subject/object, self/other, mind/body opposites that we rely on for shaping our reality have no role to play. Process is a metaperspective that joins seeming opposites into seamless fields of experience. Within this unified field, all entities are linked together by virtue of the fact that they are equal participants in the larger process.

Process philosophy describes a world that is like the Net itself—a vast, nonlinear reality wherein each node connects to every other node in an endless, recursive web. One of the major challenges inherent in embracing the sacred aspect of cyberspace is to learn to understand the world in terms of webs, nets, and circles—vast feedback loops that create themselves in an ever-unfolding pattern of emergent novelty. In the process view, as in cyberspace, we are spiders weaving webs that merge with other webs that merge with other webs in an endless ebb and flow of being and becoming.

In our journey toward a theology of cyberspace, we will begin in an arcane corner of the world of process philosophy. This is the school of process theology, a realm peopled by men and women who have taken their understanding of process and amplified it into a complete sacred vision. This group, which is not large, has existed on the periphery of various disciplines for several decades. These thinkers are too philosophical for most theologians, too interested in the divine to please mainstream philosophers, and are always flirting with the areas where science and theology cross. Process theologians have tended to fall through the cracks. But this has not deterred those for whom the process vision is simply the best articulation of the world as they see it. Among the more prominent of those who have dedicated their lives to pursuing this iconoclastic vision is John B. Cobb, Jr.[1]

Raised by Methodist missionaries in Japan and the southern state of Georgia, Cobb's early experiences in academia can be seen as paradigmatic for many thinking people in the West. He entered the halls of learning as a devout Christian whose faith in God was unquestioned. Within months, this faith was utterly shattered and, in his words, "his prayers bounced back from the ceiling unheard." Cobb found that he could not reconcile the God of his youth with the powerful ideas he was exposed to at university. Freud, Darwin, and the pantheon of modernist Western intellectuals revealed to him a world that had no need for God. At this point, Cobb underwent a crisis not unlike one that many of us experience. His early ideas of divinity were exposed as naive and simplistic. For Cobb, this experience spelled not an end but a beginning. He elected the difficult task of synthesizing the intellectual and the spiritual. In this quest, Cobb stumbled onto the legacy of the English philosopher Alfred North Whitehead.

Whitehead, considered by many the greatest Western thinker since Plato, had trained as a mathematician. His first major work, undertaken while still living in England, was an enormous effort, coauthored with Bertrand Russell, titled *Principia Mathematica*. This treatise was an attempt to devise a philosophy of mathematics based on logic. In Whitehead's view, this work failed miserably. What *Principia Mathematica* revealed to Whitehead was that logic could not fully explain the fundamental nature of reality. The world we live in, Whitehead concluded, ultimately contained a nonlogical element, what he called a "God-shaped hole." With this understanding, Whitehead turned his attention to deciphering the qualities more fundamental than logic that underlie the universe. Toward the end of his life, while in residence at

---

1. No relation to the author.

Harvard University in the 1920s and 1930s, Whitehead wrote his magnum opus, *Process and Reality*. It is the radical philosophical vision contained in this work that Whitehead's intellectual descendants would come to call "process philosophy."

Whitehead's speculative philosophy appealed to Cobb at the deepest levels of his being. Here was an entirely rational, coherent view of the universe that depended on a divine reality. This divinity was utterly unlike any Cobb had previously experienced, and yet it filled the place left vacant by his intellectual awakening—that of a divine force fully integrated into the whole of his life. Central to Cobb's previous faith experience was a belief that the world needed the divine in order to be understood at its deepest levels. After discovering Whitehead, he experienced a return to that place of divine meaning, but with a much more sophisticated perspective. As he would write many years later, "Very gradually, I began putting my world back together or, more accurately, constructing a new one, because, of course, I could not go home again."

Strange bedfellows at best are John Cobb, a diminutive, soft-spoken southerner with a penetrating gaze, and the modern phenomenon of cyberspace. Cobb, a theologian who has devoted much of his career to articulating a process-based environmental theology, has only the most rudimentary understanding of computer technology. But as the outline of his Whiteheadian cosmology will make clear, there is much power in his vision for the task at hand.

On my first visit with Cobb, who had recently retired from most of his formal duties, we met in the modest single-story home that he and his wife share in Claremont, California. As I drove up to the house, located in a tasteful, older development near the college, I noticed that the front porch was dripping with plant life. This felt entirely appropriate for a man whose primary interest over the years has been ecological. The pots overflowing with lush, green life were thriving from careful attention in the balmy climate.

The front door opened quickly and Cobb ushered me into a small living room decorated with the artifacts of an academic life. As the room demonstrated, Cobb and his wife are not acquisitive people. The furnishings were comfortable yet simple. Cobb took his place in an easy chair and motioned for me to take a seat on the couch. For the next three hours, we engaged in an intensive discussion. A gentle, thoughtful man, Cobb radiates an intellectual intensity fired by a deep sense of caring for the universe. Throughout our conversation, his energy was unflagging, and I noticed in particular his ability to keep his train of thought perfectly intact, regardless of the various inevitable interruptions.

Cobb, who has spent years walking among the boundaries of disciplines, knows better than most how loaded the term "God" can be in our culture. I also am no stranger to this phenomenon. I was recently at a scientific conference where one of the keynote speakers referred to the term jokingly as "the three-letter word." "God" is so fraught with disparate meanings as to become, at best, meaningless, and at worst, a term used to dismiss derogatorily a whole realm of inquiry. Cobb has met this challenge head-on, having found a number of ways to talk about the process perspective of divinity that avoid the God trap. Among his most powerful and clear articulations is of the divine as the force of life itself.

Life as a sacred, cosmic force is a rich and complex notion, filled with far-reaching implications. First and most fundamental is the understanding that the very essence of life is process. When life ceases its becoming, its never-ending evolution, it is no longer life. Life can be identified by the moment-by-moment unfolding of creativity.

Life is the only counterentropic force that we know of in the universe. In other words, while most of the universe is rushing headlong into a state of chaotic dispersal, life works to create order, complexity, and richly diverse experience. Life is that which can incorporate infinite potential into itself. Life achieves this awesome feat through the continual manifestation of novelty. Creative transformation is the hallmark of life.

Creativity, the very essence of the divine, is the life-giving principle that is also itself alive, moving, changing and growing. On the simplest level, divinity is the cosmic force that continually ushers novelty and creativity into the world. The divine is not the process but the creative aspect of the process. From this perspective, the transcendent aspect of divinity is pure, unmanifest creativity or pure potential. The immanent aspect, that part we can apprehend in the world around us, manifests as creative novelty and richness of experience. Wherever creativity is found, there too can life be found.

At this point, *life* itself becomes a slippery term. Are we to conclude that the divine power of creativity is limited to living matter? Not at all, Cobb argues. In fact, he states, "The power of life is not limited to clearly living things, and we may think of life as exerting its gentle pressure everywhere, encouraging each thing to become more than it is."[2]

In other words, creativity can be found suffused throughout the evolutionary spectrum of becoming.

The view of life as a continuum of expression is today embraced by many biologists. Life extends, for some, from the quasi-alive virus on up to humans, and in some cases, beyond. Cobb's view opens this definition even wider. For Cobb, as for Whitehead, there can be elements of creative novelty in what we would consider inanimate things. There

---

2. Charles Birch and John B. Cobb, Jr., *The Liberation of Life*, page 189.

can be flashes of novelty in atoms and molecules. In the case of things such as rocks, the creativity does not happen at the level of the whole object. A rock will not move of its own accord. However, the constituent parts of the rock, its molecular particles, can exhibit moments of creative change. In this sense, nothing is truly exempt from participating in the larger flow of divine, creative life through the universe.

In claiming that no clear boundaries can be drawn between the animate and the inanimate, Cobb is not affirming the vitalist doctrine that life is a discrete substance. Instead, he is arguing that there exists in the universe a continuity between all things, and that the essence of that continuity is divine novelty. Cobb explains, "There is no such *thing* as life. For different purposes the line may be drawn at different places. Or, better still, if people can get used to the idea, all such line drawing may cease. We have a widely varied set of entities which manifest in varying degrees and under varying circumstances different features which are associated with living things. Any line is arbitrary."[3]

Novelty in this context does not mean mere change. Change is the basic feature of entropy, whereas, as Cobb says, "novelty is the possibility for a specific kind of change, a type which runs counter to the vast movements of change in the universe."[4] Novelty occurs when the present moment transcends the past in some significant way through a creative synthesis. This idea of novelty depends rather strongly on an embrace of nondeterministic forces. In a strictly deterministic model, each moment will appear to carry forward the influences of the past moment—no more, no less. However, when novelty enters the picture, the present moment transcends the past to become more than it once was. This, according to Cobb, forms the very essence of life. It is also

3. Ibid., page 93.

4. Ibid., page 184.

the essence of divinity. In Whitehead's somewhat denser language, "The essence of life is the teleological introduction of novelty, with some conformation of objectives. Thus novelty of circumstances is met with novelty of functioning adapted to steadiness of purpose."[5]

Another term for "novelty," and one that is not limited to our traditional understandings of life, is *emergence*. Emergent behavior, as I have noted previously, is strictly defined as any situation where the whole is greater than the sum of its parts. There are many examples of emergence, some of which constitute the greatest mysteries of science. How did the universe begin? How is it that life emerged from nonlife? Consciousness from mere sentience? In the 1920s, Lloyd Morgan, in his book *Emergent Evolution,* called these occurrences "miracles" because they could not be explained by physics or chemistry.[6] Morgan held that when these miracles occurred, new laws above and beyond those outlined by classical science were born. The difficulty with this view is that it explains nothing about how such miracles can happen. The idea of emergence has traditionally been nothing more than a placeholder for mystery.

The understanding of emergent qualities has continued to defy the greatest scientific minds of our time. Perhaps this is because science alone cannot provide the whole answer. To fully understand emergence, it may be that one must incorporate the mechanistic truths of science into a larger framework that takes into account the nonmechanical patterns of connection between all things. Truth, in this context, is found not just in the stuff of the world but in the ways in which the stuff is related, connected, and woven together.

Computers are infused with emergence, with novelty, with life as

---

5. As quoted in ibid., page 109.

6. As cited in ibid., page 78.

Cobb understands it. The Internet and the World Wide Web constitute a vast, self-organizing, emergent phenomenon defined on one level by hardware and software, but on another level by patterns of behavior and the process of unfolding. In the more rarefied realms of artificial life and emergent artificial intelligence, scientists and researchers are purposively using the mysterious force of emergence to evolve new computer code and systems that have no predictable outcome. The secret key to understanding this force of emergence, of novelty, is not to be found in arcane mathematical formulae or scientific systems theory. The kernel of the mystery resides in the world of the divine.

FEEDBACK LOOPS

Does this mean that computers are alive? Certainly not in any conventional sense. But when life is viewed as an expression of novelty, computers begin to exhibit some rudimentary lifelike qualities. Kevin Kelly, editor of *Wired* magazine, has explored this topic extensively in his book *Out of Control.* Kelly has been writing about the world of computers for many years, tracking their deployment into the world through his unique and eclectic viewpoint. Through his research on computers and his examination of cybernetic arcana such as feedback loops, Kelly has arrived at a view of life closely related to Cobb's.

"Aliveness is a continuum and some things are more alive than others," Kelly states. "I think that the Net might be getting as close to being alive as a virus. What does that mean? It is certainly not conscious. But it has some adaptability, some self-healing abilities, it has biological growth. So it's a little alive."

When Kelly talks about what life is, a common theme begins

to emerge. For Kelly, life is fundamentally "a process that makes the process itself become richer over time. I would describe life as a process that creates its own environment to create more varieties of itself. Within this is the germ of an idea that life is a self-causing agent, it's something that is not just causing itself, but is causing the possibility space in which it exists."

What Kelly is pointing to here is a fundamental theological concept—at the root of life is the tautology or paradox that life creates itself. In the same vein, the divine has no beginning and no end but is an endless loop of cosmic power. God is uncreated. Life is also uncreated. It is, as Kelly points out, both "source and fruition." In other words, life is both the ground of its own being as well as the source of its ongoing creativity.

In the process view, the divine as life both generates the forward movement of the process as well as gathers and includes into itself the whole of the process. As life continues to create increasing order and complexity, the whole that the divine includes is larger, richer, and has more creative potential. Therefore, the process of the divine manifesting itself in the world is marked by an ongoing enlargement of the space for its own expression. According to Kelly, this is also precisely what life, evolution—and ultimately cyberspace—are doing.

"The process of evolution is about exploring all the possible processes," Kelly states. "It is actually making the possibility space larger. That's what technology is about, that is what thinking is about, that is what life in general is about. It's not just that we have a space and we are trying to create all the possible artifacts in that space that we can. Life is doing something in that space that suddenly enlarges that space out of what came before."

Kelly arrived at this definition of life by looking deeply into the world of cybernetics, a field whose theories are foundational to the creation of the computers we use today. Kelly began his exploration with the father of cybernetics, Norbert Weiner, a wunderkind professor of mathematics who also studied with Bertrand Russell. In his groundbreaking book, *Cybernetics,* Weiner introduced the fundamental computational idea of feedback loops.

Feedback loops are deceptively simple circuits that link one or more parts of a system, establishing a rudimentary informational exchange. For example, the toilet, a mechanism that Kelly calls a "prototypical cybernetic example." Many toilets contain a simple knob that can be adjusted for various water levels in the tank. When this knob is set, it tells a self-regulating mechanism in the tank to adjust the water level. Imagine that a second self-regulating mechanism is connected to turn the knob automatically. This second loop "senses the water pressure in the feed pipe and then moves the knob so that it assigns a high level to the toilet when there is high water pressure and a lower level when the pressure is low."[7] In other words, a simple feedback loop is born.

Simple loops such as these can be linked together in an almost infinite chain within a given system. But when more than one loop is in play, something odd begins to emerge. We see that, as Kelly writes, "A triggers B, and B triggers C, and C triggers A. In outright paradox, A is both cause and effect. Cybernetician Heinz von Foerster called this elusive cycle 'circular causality.' . . . Hackers know it as a recursive circuit. Whatever the riddle is called, it flies in the face of 3,000 years of logical philosophy. It undermines classical everything. If something can be both its own cause and effect, then rationality is up for grabs."[8]

Computers are riddled with feedback loops, with self-generating

---

7. Kevin Kelly, *Out of Control,* page 123.
8. Ibid.

paradoxes of becoming. This tiny, seemingly insignificant key forms a crucial bridge between the divine and computer technology. The feedback loop manifests the self-generating quality that is a hallmark of divine creativity and spiritual evolution. What is remarkable about this little loop is that it reveals to us that one of the most fundamental aspects of divinity—the process of creating more process, of self-transcendence and self-organization—is found not only in life but can manifest at the level of the machine.

The feedback loop is an extremely minor example of divine creative power in action. This understanding of divinity does not mean that there exists an all-powerful, supernatural force exerting influence from on high on lowly feedback loops. The source of the self-generating creativity found in feedback loops is divine creative novelty.

The divine as creative process does not exert efficient cause on the world or hold the special place of final cause, as some traditional theologies teach. This is because there is no divine causality in a linear sense, only the never-ending emergence of novelty. The divine is not the absolute ruler and creator of the universe. Instead, the divine manifests an *uncreated* creative power—a continuous, persuasive force that coaxes richness and order to grow in the universe. There was no time when creativity as embodied by divinity did not exist. This is not to say that the particular cosmic epoch in which we now live, generally thought to have begun with a big bang, had no beginning. As Whitehead writes, "The creation of the world is the incoming of a type of order establishing a cosmic epoch. It is not the beginning of matter of fact, but the incoming of a certain type of social order." The divine is the cosmic force that brings order out of chaos through the workings of creative events. This is precisely the force that is playing itself out in the simple feedback loop popularized by Weiner.

THE MANY BECOME ONE AND ARE INCREASED BY ONE

In order to understand at a deeper level the unfolding of the divine in systems as simple as the feedback loop and as complex as evolution itself, we must spend some time understanding the inner workings of Whitehead's metaphysics. According to Whitehead, creativity forms the ultimate reality of the universe. The transcendent aspect of divinity is pure creativity. All things that can be found in the world are generated in part by divine creativity made manifest. This does not mean that everything is simply an instance of the divine. What it means is that all things include divine creativity in the process of coming into being.

In Whitehead's view, the world is not composed of different types of things. Instead, the universe is made up of one primary quality—process—that differs not in kind but in degree. For example, it may appear to us that bodies and minds are radically different entities. But for Whitehead, bodies and minds are both instances of process working itself through substrates that appear distinct only from a materialist perspective. From the process perspective, both mind and body are fundamentally expressions of the same reality. Whitehead's term for the basic metaphysical units that constitute this reality is "occasions of experience." In other words, each entity is not a "thing," like a body or even a thought, but a moment of experience. The rapid unfolding of sequential moments of experience is what generates the objective reality that we call bodies and minds.

Whitehead's use of the term *experience* can be a bit confusing. Experience does not mean consciousness or self-consciousness. His intention in using this term is to highlight the process inherent in each moment as opposed to the outcome. For example, a table is not an object. If we examine a table in each moment, we find that it is composed of a dynamic flux of energy in the form of atoms. These atoms too are composed of dynamic process; they are occasions of experience. The table as a whole is understood as an aggregate of these individual occasions.

Whitehead's belief that the universe is composed of a single metaphysical process that appears in different forms is analogous to the scientific understanding that the laws of the universe, once discovered, are applicable to all of reality. Gravity as a law applies as equally to a mountaintop as to the bottom of the sea. The difference between Whitehead and traditional science is that Whitehead begins his analysis not from a mechanistic perspective but from the perspective of human experience. This position, argues Whitehead, is the only place we honestly can start from. All of our understandings will necessarily be colored by our experience of the world.

Experience is, by definition, subjective. Therefore, Whitehead concludes subjective experience must be a general feature of the universe. Whitehead's occasions of experience refer to the subjective participation of each entity in its surrounding environment. The nature and structure of an atom is not an immutable state, determined since the beginning of time. Indeed, as quantum physics has demonstrated, there are no such objective "things" as atoms. Atoms are both particles and waves.

Researchers at the National Institute of Standards and Technology recently gathered experimental evidence for this weird truth when they were able to take a single ion of beryllium and make it spin both clockwise and counterclockwise at the same time. Reporting on this momentous experiment in the *New York Times*, writer George Johnson asked the key question: When does this odd quantum effect solidify into the objects that we think of as real? He found the most popular answer was as follows: "Once the electron brushes against something else, its two states come unstuck and we're left with an electron that is spinning one way or the other." In other words, the paradox of the ion spinning both ways at the same time resolves. Johnson explains that for any given object, the atoms are "constantly interacting with one another and with the surrounding atmosphere—all these tiny, inanimate 'observations' anchoring it in the land of either-or."[9] This experiment begins to hint at Whitehead's metaphysics. The electrons "observe" their environment, and this tells them which way to spin. Whitehead argues that all actual entities in the world are "observers" who become what they are through participating in their environment.

The counterintuitive premise that the world is fundamentally made up of events unfolding in time also fits quite neatly with the Einsteinian notion of relativity.[10] In his revolutionary theory, $E=MC^2$, Einstein pointed out two foundational ideas. First, energy and mass are convertible. Second, the relativity between energy and matter depends on the existence of a spatio-temporal domain. In other words, in the reality to which we wake every morning, our basic field of experience, matter is an instantiation of energy within space and *time*. Time, or process, is a crucial piece of the whole.

The contemporary field of consciousness studies also sheds some light on Whitehead's view. It is a well-respected notion among some observers of consciousness that the world we apprehend is not the objective, pregiven reality. Rather, consciousness is a subjective process

9. George Johnson, "On Skinning Schrödinger's Cat," *New York Times* Week in Review, June 2, 1996, page 16.

10. Einstein, in his famous statement that God doesn't play dice, himself never fully accepted the principles of quantum mechanics. It is important to note here that these two examples, quantum and relativity physics, constitute two distinct and, on some level, contradictory views of the physical world. The process view can find support from both perspectives.

that cocreates reality in concert with the inputs of the world on a moment-by-moment basis. Research by Roger Penrose and Stuart Hameroff points to a quantum basis for consciousness wherein awareness arises and dissipates out of the quantum flux. This view has much in common with the ancient wisdom that comes from the meditative religious traditions. Very advanced Buddhist meditators report reaching states of awareness wherein they become aware of their consciousness forming itself.[11] This formation takes the shape of extremely rapid kernels of consciousness that come into being and quickly pass away, almost like frames in a film. The duration of these frames is hotly debated, but in general they are thought to be on the order of milliseconds. These frames can be likened to Whitehead's occasions of experience, playing out in the realm of human consciousness.

Whitehead's metaphysics turns on its head the modernist assumption that the world is made up of individual, unchanging objects. As he wrote in *Adventures of Ideas*, "Such an account of the ultimate atom, or of the ultimate monad, renders an interconnected world unintelligible. The universe is shivered into a multitude of disconnected substantial things, each thing in its own way exemplifying its private bundle of abstract characters which have found a home in its own substantial individuality. But substantial thing cannot call unto substantial thing."[12] In other words, if our fundamental experience of the universe is process, or change, it is foolish to reduce reality to discrete objects that do not change. The challenge for Whitehead was to explain how certain patterns appear to remain constant in a world characterized by constant flux.

Whitehead divided his occasions of experience into two distinct

---

11. See Wilber, Engler, and Brown, *Transformations of Consciousness*.

12. As quoted in Jeremy Hayward, *Perceiving Ordinary Magic*, page 227.

aspects that he called the physical pole and the mental pole. The physical pole makes the most sense to those of us schooled in the modernist scientific tradition. On its simplest level, this is the aspect of an event that absorbs influences from the past. The physical pole is an occasion's receptive state. According to the type of event or occasion that is being examined, this pole will have varying degrees of influence. At what we think of as the inanimate level, where emergent behavior is highly unlikely, the physical pole dominates. For example, the moment-by-moment experience of a molecule is almost wholly determined by the context of its previous occasion—where it exists in space, what other molecules it is near. In this case, the physical pole plays a primary role. From this perspective it is easy to understand why traditional, physical sciences—which prefer to understand reality based on the smallest, physical components they can find—would conclude that the world is made up of different types of things, not, as Whitehead argues, events that contain different proportions of two primary poles. At the molecular and atomic levels, the world does appear to be made up of discrete objects. The flashes of creativity that do exist can be written off as anomalies.

Whitehead's second pole, the mental pole, is something of a misnomer; it naturally leads one to believe he is referring to conscious mentality. In fact, he means something much subtler. Just as the physical pole can be thought of as the receptive element, that which receives from the past, the mental pole can be thought of as that element of an event that *integrates* information from the past with the alternative possibilities or creative potential in any given moment. It is through the mental pole that events participate subjectively in their environment.

The mental pole operates on an unconscious, instinctive level. By the time a moment of creative novelty reaches our consciousness, the moment of creative synthesis has already passed. This does not mean that the mental pole is limited to the unconscious aspect of conscious beings. The mental pole operates at every level of reality, in every occasion of experience. It is present, for example, in the feedback loop. Without the loop having any experience that we would call sentient, it is capable of integrating novelty into itself and then passing that information on down the line. Were it not capable of this, it would not *be* a feedback loop. The feedback loop's integrative ability, its mental pole, is the aspect of it that manifests the tautology inherent in its nature. The ability to respond creatively to the environment leads to self-generativity. Once something can generate its own novelty, it can begin to define its own possibility space.

Whitehead's occasions of experience, which he also called "actual entities," all contain the quality of self-generativity found in the feedback loop. Whitehead called this phenomenon "self-movement" and posited that it could be found at every level of nature, from atoms to molecules to humans. The self-movement generated by the mental pole is a basic, metaphysical law of the universe. If this is true, it should not surprise us to see this ability beginning to move into the world of computation. Cyberspace, with its silicon-based hardware and mathematics-based software, offers a new realm for self-generativity to explore.

Although all self-moving actual entities include both the physical and the mental, the mental may not always produce novelty. In many instances, the mental pole will lead to a repetition of what has been. In fact, Whitehead makes a crucial distinction at this juncture between actual, self-moving individuals and what he calls "aggregates of individuals," such as a table. Most inanimate things, such as a rock or a telephone pole, are not occasions of experience. They are composed of billions of individual events, each of which constitutes a self-moving occasion of experience. But the whole of the rock demonstrates no creative power; its creative experience is contained in the elements that constitute it.

Individual events occur at every level of nature, from the subatomic to the atomic, the molecular, the cellular, and up to the human mind. As we move up the ladder of being, from the atomic world to the realm of what we traditionally think of as the living, we can observe a basic shift in the balance between the two poles. At the level of the atom, the physical pole pretty much rules the day.[13] But once we leave the realm of classical physics and enter the realm of biology, this balance shifts quickly. Even in the simplest, single-celled organism, it becomes much more difficult to determine what the future will bring. In this realm, the mental pole of creative synthesis presents itself more clearly. Will the cell ooze this way or that, absorb its nutrients through this section of cell wall, or pass by looking for other food? By the time we reach the level of the human, the mental pole is fully evident. As Cobb explained, "Mind, or psyche, or the soul, is the place where novelty is most intensively nurtured and developed. This novelty affects what takes place in the rest of the body and influences future novelty. Therefore, with regard to life, the soul is in some sense even more alive than an individual cell in the body."

Whiteheadian reality is composed of discrete moments wherein a complex of forces come together simultaneously. Therefore, although the occasions of experience unfold in time, they should be thought of as nontemporal wholes. Each moment arises from an active process of self-creativity. It then becomes an object, which the next moment can receive and integrate as it undergoes its own process of self-creativity. The universe is a steady stream of these moments unfolding in time.

---

13. At the subatomic level, the level of quantum, the balance, of course, shifts again, quite radically. Quantum mechanics, as Roger Penrose points out, has much coherence with Whitehead's idea of the world being comprised of "occasions of experience." For more on Penrose's view, see Stuart Hameroff and Roger Penrose, "Conscious Events as Orchestrated Space-Time Selections," *Journal of Consciousness Studies* 3, no. 1, 1996, pages 36–53.

We can now begin to understand Whitehead's famous dictum, "The many become one and are increased by one." With this statement, Whitehead summarized his basic metaphysical outlook. Each moment, each actual entity, receives multiple influences from the past (the many), which it incorporates into the present moment (become one) and, simultaneously, synthesizes new experience from the infinite well of divine creative potential (and are increased by one). For Whitehead, as for Cobb, every individual actual occasion, from the atom to the human, is composed of an ever-changing balance of both physical and mental, receptive and integrative energy.

Cyberspace offers a wholly new terrain for contemplating Whitehead's system. As we have seen, one of the simplest foundations of computing, the feedback loop, embodies the metaphysics of self-generative novelty. When these loops are put into the context of computer systems, a whole new order begins to happen. A space of pure process is born. In cyberspace, the creative, self-generative properties of the universe are laid bare for us to experience. There is no material stuff, no matter, to blind us to the essential processes of the universe. This is not to say that cyberspace offers a world unconstrained by the material. Both the hardware and the software are vital to the process, as is the larger context of human agency that cyberspace is born from and reflects in an ongoing way. Rather, cyberspace begins to lift the modernist veil from our eyes as it reveals that events in time form the heart not only of its reality but of the larger world into which it is woven.

THEOLOGICAL CREATIVITY IN ACTION

Cyberspace was born from and continues to depend on human consciousness for its very existence. We created it, we shape it, we use it.

Even so, there is an aspect of it that remains beyond our control. Cyberspace may be our creation, but it is more appropriate to think of it as an extension of divine creativity working through the medium of human consciousness. The connective tissue between it and us is our mutual participation in the ongoing creative unfolding of the divine. As we usher the emerging world of cyberspace into being, we are co-participating in the sacred forces of the universe.

Tuning ourselves to this unique perspective means learning to trust the sometimes mysterious process of theological creativity. This process does not affirm the idea of the divine as a purely good entity from an anthropomorphic perspective, exerting control on a sinful humanity from on high. The divine as theological creativity gave birth to life and to consciousness, both of which have been responsible for untold suffering in the world. In light of this, the goodness of the sacred takes a new form. As Cobb says, "The emergence of life is also responsible for the emergence of suffering and mutual destruction. You have to say that God is responsible for that. So the question of whether one affirms God as good is a function of whether you believe life is, in spite of all the suffering that comes with it, something wonderful and valuable. And it's possible to take the view that the suffering that comes with life is so terrible that it would have been better to have nothing at all. Whether God is good or not is basically a function not of a just or virtuous creation, but a decision that it's better to live than not to live."

Theologian David Griffin elaborates on this central idea when he writes, "The portrayal of the world as a web of centers of creative experience leads to a quite different notion of holy power. . . . Power is threefold. It is, first, the ability to receive the offerings of others creatively, which is receptive power. It is, second, the ability to transcend the power of others and to make a partially self-determining response (for example, forgiveness), which is self-creative power. It is, third, the ability to influence others creatively, so as to maximize their own creativity, which is the power of persuasion or evocation. This third type of power is the type of relational power that God has. . . . God's power to influence us is just that—the power to *influence,* to enter into us, and thereby to evoke the highest receptive, self-creative, and persuasive power in us."[14]

Theological creativity is that which lures us always toward a deeper, more complex, and ultimately purposeful and loving outcome. This lure forms a common ground of wholeness, leading to an ethic of participation in a deeply interconnected world. The heart of this ethic is the interplay between the receptive and creative forces of the cosmic wholeness. The divine calls us to integrate possibility, particularly those potentials that will lead to a richer and more creative environment for all. Spiritual development and growth is an always-waiting invitation. It is incumbent upon us to bring it into our lives.

When we approach the universe with a fundamental belief in its sacred creative nature, we allow ourselves to be transformed into richer, more deeply connected, whole, and loving beings. As we reach into our own most alive place—our souls—to connect with the divine wholeness, we can begin to bring the unconscious divine process of creative novelty into conscious manifestation. When this happens, we experience an awareness of the divine plan and our place within it. Cyberspace has much to teach us as it tunes our awareness to the ways in which divinity flows into each and every aspect of creation.

---

14. David Ray Griffin, *God & Religion in the Postmodern World,* page 48.

(3)

THE MIND OF GOD

In early 1995, the French bishop Jacques Gaillot claimed a unique place in history. He became the first virtual bishop, tending to the wired masses from a Web site. This turn of events was not something that Gaillot had anticipated or planned for. He undertook the unexpected migration to cyberspace after having made himself somewhat unwelcome to the powers that be within the hierarchy of the Vatican.

In 1994, Bishop Gaillot, a soft-spoken man who oversaw the diocese of Évreux, in Normandy, became deeply involved in the fate of a group of squatters living in an abandoned building on Paris's chic Left Bank. In France, being homeless means more than simply being reduced to living on the streets. Homelessness in France is quite rare and deeply embarrassing to the French psyche. To be homeless is to literally be "excluded," to be marginalized in the strictest social and political sense. When it comes to the homeless, most of us just don't want to know.

Bishop Gaillot was appalled by the lack of concern displayed by the French authorities for the fate of these people. Gaillot, along with several other members of the clergy, threw himself into the issue, becoming a highly visible and outspoken advocate for the civil rights of the homeless. Soon, he was living with the squatters, drawing enormous media attention to their plight and, simultaneously, to his own viewpoint on the matter. The Catholic Church in France was not amused by these proceedings, and in January 1995, Bishop Gaillot was summoned to Rome for a meeting with the pope.

After that fateful meeting, Bishop Gaillot was informed that his function as a bishop in Evreux had come to an end and that his see was to be declared vacant beginning the next day at noon. Bishop Gaillot refused, putting the Church hierarchy in a difficult position. A bishop cannot be fired and there were no real grounds for excommunication. The rules of the Church forbade the pope from demoting him. Further, the pope was required by Church law to give Bishop Gaillot a place to be the bishop of. For several months, Bishop Gaillot heard nothing. Then, in the fall of 1995, he received a letter announcing that he had been transferred to the see of Partenia. Bishop Gaillot searched the maps of France, looking for Partenia. His efforts were in vain. Not only was Partenia not located in France, it barely existed at all.

In the fourth century, Partenia, which is currently located somewhere in Algeria, had been an important diocese. But times change, and since the sixth century, Partenia had been little more than a heap of sand dunes somewhere in the northern Sahara. Even so, the see had never been abolished. It thus became the perfect resting place for the troublesome Gaillot. The same rules that bound the pope to give Gaillot a see also bound Bishop Gaillot to accept it. Gaillot officially became the bishop of Partenia.

When Leo Sheer, a French intellectual and the author of the book *Virtual Democracy*, got wind of Bishop Gaillot's situation, he had a brainstorm. Why not put the see of Partenia on-line? "Instead of a metaphysical idea of a bishop, attached to a real place, we would have a metaphysical idea of a place attached to a real bishop," Scheer commented. For Sheer, the idea of a virtual bishop resonated beautifully with the inherent qualities of cyberspace. He said, "The mind of God is imitated by the virtual structure of the Internet, where the difference between the physical actuality and real existence has at last been breached."[1]

Partenia quickly attracted both media attention in France and a worldwide following of participants from Australia to Africa and America. Bishop Gaillot had found a new platform from which to spread his version of the social gospel. Partenia included links to a wide variety of French and international aid organizations as well as a host of religious sites ranging from Buddhist to Catholic. As Bishop Gaillot wrote in a March 1996 letter posted on the Partenia Web site, "The Internet is a means of communication; the team which has gathered around me wishes it to be at the service and even at the disposal of those who are excluded from the mainstream society, so that they can speak for themselves and may find an answer to their questions."[2]

Although Bishop Gaillot seems to have accepted his new position as a virtual bishop with enormous equanimity, the deeper meaning of his role in history has not escaped him. In an interview with writer Adam Gopnik he commented, "The primitive Church was a kind of Internet itself, which was one of the reasons it was so difficult for the Roman Empire to combat it. The early Christians understood that what was most important was not to claim physical power in a physical place but to establish a network of believers—to be on line. I think of Paul, for instance, when he had to decide whether to travel to Jerusalem or

---

1. Adam Gopnik, *The New Yorker*, March 18, 1996, page 61.

2. A letter from Jacques Gaillot, March 1, 1996, available at: http://www.partenia.org

Rome, and chose instead to go to Asia Minor—to sidestep the vertical hierarchy by moving horizontally. The church has always prospered when it moves horizontally and suffered when it becomes locked vertically."[3]

Through cyberspace, the bishop can move horizontally, communicating in a wholly new way the issues of the excluded. After all, for more than a thousand years Partenia existed primarily in the virtual space of God's mind. Now it exists in a new, virtual realm, but one that manages to communicate the resolutely nonvirtual needs of marginalized groups. As Bishop Gaillot said, "You know the strangest thing about Partenia? It is that I have probably been there. Physically, I mean. I did my military service in Algeria, many years ago. It's possible that at some time or other I drove through Partenia and saw the diocese where I would become bishop—which then existed in the mind of God, and now exists as a series of electrons racing through the world. Once the spirit enters the world, anything is possible."[4]

As the story of Bishop Gaillot illustrates, the divine novelty inherent in cyberspace can serve an evolutionary social function, enabling spiritual and political work to unfold in new ways. The see of Partenia defies the limitations of time and space while retaining the ability to serve as a source of spiritual sustenance for those who participate in it. The virtual diocese carries forth the ancient urge for spiritual community in an utterly new context. The extension of spiritual experience into global domains such as this may well be a natural part of the trajectory of evolution. Virtual spaces release a new energy into our cultural and social spheres of experience, an energy that contains some important spiritual insights.

---

3. Adam Gopnik, *The New Yorker,* March 18, 1996, page 63.
4. Ibid.

GUiDED EVOLUTiOn

The context of the virtual see, as Marshall McLuhan's famous dictum "the medium is the message" so clearly reminds us, carries a powerful significance. The medium of cyberspace opens the door to a new level of evolutionary activity fueled by spirit. To reach a deeper understanding of how computers are weaving themselves through certain aspects of our sacred experience, we turn to the work of another French Catholic priest, who worked several decades before computing became ubiquitous. This man's name was Pierre Teilhard de Chardin, and his unique philosophical blending of science and theology offers a key to the deeper meaning of stories like Bishop Gaillot's. Interestingly, an important turning point in Teilhard's own journey also transpired on the North African sands.

Teilhard, a Jesuit and a paleontologist, felt strongly the pull of the divine embedded in the material world. This pull was confusing for him. As a Jesuit, the pantheistic notion of a material basis for the divine was deeply heretical. To complicate matters, Teilhard had also had deep, personal experiences of a transcendent divinity that existed far beyond the physical world. These two seemingly opposed experiences raised profound questions in him. Which was the real God—the one he felt in the rocks he dug for his science, or the one of the Church? The reconciliation of these two seemingly paradoxical manifestations of spirit would consume his prodigious energies throughout his long life. Ultimately, Teilhard came to understand these two Gods as one, joined together in the larger process of spiritual evolution. From this fundamental insight, Teilhard would produce multiple philosophical treatises that daringly blended science and theology in a coherent worldview that, oddly enough, was utterly prescient about the coming of cyberspace.

From his earliest boyhood Teilhard was drawn in two opposing directions—toward the spirituality of the Church and the solidity of science. One of his first memories was of "sitting at the age of five by the fireplace at Sarcenat while his mother cut his hair. Under her scissors, a snippet fell into the fire, darkened, and disappeared. The child was seized with horror and disgust. What was disappearing, he suddenly realized, was a part of himself—curling like an autumn leaf, turning into nothing. 'An awful feeling came on me at that moment,' he later wrote. 'For the first time in my life I knew that I was perishable.' "[5] Thus, at the tender age of five, Teilhard came face to face with his mortality.

Teilhard sought to allay the deep fear that this realization produced in him by collecting bits of iron, a substance he believed to be permanent. He came to call these scraps his "God of iron." When at the age of ten he discovered a bit of rust on the surface of a plow, terror came over him once again. At that moment, he discovered rocks, which he decided were the most permanent aspect of creation. While he was later to see the fallacy of this assumption, it was in this early impulse for lasting security that Teilhard's lifelong love for matter had its roots.

Teilhard's love of matter found its counterbalance in his deeply pious upbringing as the fourth of eleven children from a well-to-do Catholic family in the Auvergne region of central France. Teilhard's mother was an exceptionally devout Catholic who placed worship at the center of her large family's life; regular devotionals were an integral part of his childhood. The cathedral in Clermont-Ferrand, near his home in Sarcenat, was the center of community life in an area where his family was among the most prominent citizens.

---

5. Ellen and Mary Lukas, *Teilhard: A Biography*, page 23.

All of the Teilhard boys were sent to a Jesuit school at the age of eleven and Pierre was no exception. His years as a boarder at school, where he received much attention as an exceptional student, encouraged him to deepen the other great commitment in his life—his unswerving devotion to an ineffable, transcendent, personal God.

It was at the age of eighteen that Teilhard felt most clearly the opposition of the two forces of cosmos and the divine. He was at a crossroads, trying to decide between a future as a scientist or as a Jesuit priest. He understood that these professions were, on many levels, antithetical. This was an understanding that would prove prophetic. His novice master in the Jesuit order convinced him that he could be both a Jesuit and a paleontologist. Thus assured, he entered seminary and began his lifelong, often-conflicted relationship with the Roman Catholic Church.

Teilhard's early years in seminary were spent on the isle of Jersey in the English Channel. From there he was sent to do his teaching internship in Cairo, where he taught physics and mathematics. While in Egypt, Teilhard spent many hours wandering through the desert, collecting and cataloging fossils. It was in the course of this work, for which he achieved some small notoriety, that what Teilhard would come to call his Cosmic Sense began to find its expression.

Teilhard would later write of this period, "One day I was looking out over the dreary expanse of the desert. As far as the eye could see, the purple steps of the uplands rose up in a series. . . . [O]n such occasions, maybe, I have been possessed by a great yearning to go and find, far from men and far from toil the place where dwell the vast forces that cradle us and possess us, where my overtense activity might indefinitely become more relaxed . . . there lay matter, and matter was calling to me. To me in turn, as to all the sons of man, it was speaking as every generation hears it speak; it was begging me to surrender myself unreservedly to it, and to worship it."[6]

Although the pull of a pantheistic God was strong, Teilhard resisted, knowing that the truth of his experience was more complex. Shortly thereafter, he underwent what he called his first "reversal." In that moment, Teilhard experienced matter as a mirror reflecting the ineffable. He felt himself move from the divine spark in matter back toward transcendent spirit. Through this reversal, he came to understand the continuous nature of what he formerly thought of as two separate Gods—one for the material and one for the transcendent. He now knew that the divine force was one and the same, whether embedded in matter or existing in a pure, spiritual form. It was Teilhard's willingness to recognize spirit in both the physical and the nonphysical realms, and his insistence on synthesizing these two experiences, that would lead to his singular vision of divine activity in the world.

The process of blending the two worlds in which he lived began to mature in earnest when Teilhard first read Henri Bergson,[7] the early and influential French evolutionary theorist. Bergson believed that the evolutionary process was threaded through with a force that he called the *élan vital*. This idea sparked a series of insights that coalesced for Teilhard in the centrality of the idea of evolution. Evolution became the bridge concept that enabled him to articulate his experience of a continuous divine force throughout creation. As Teilhard would later

---

6. From "Cosmic Life," as quoted in John Grim, *Teilhard de Chardin*, page 31.

7. Bergson's theories are now widely discredited because of his reliance on a vitalist perspective that was profoundly dualist in nature. In essence, vitalism split "life" from "matter," deeming the life force, Bergson's élan vital, as a stand-alone component of the universe. Though deeply influenced by Bergson's idea of an invisible force in the evolutionary process, Teilhard would ultimately reject his inherent dualist tendencies.

write, "Is evolution a theory, a system or a hypothesis? It is much more: it is a general condition to which all theories, all hypotheses, all systems must bow and which they must satisfy henceforward if they are to be thinkable and true. Evolution is a light illuminating all facts, a curve that all lines must follow."[8]

The concept of evolution allowed Teilhard to frame his mystical vision of matter imbued with a divine force in the fundamental truth that all things are in process. For Teilhard, this meant that matter was not antithetical to the divine, but essentially vitalized by it. He saw that the "All" was in fact ultraliving. This was a radical turning point that led Teilhard to formulate a vision of evolution as led, ultimately, by divinity. For him, evolution was both a scientific and a holy process.

In keeping with Whitehead's philosophy, Teilhard believed that all things, living or not, contain the seeds of life and consciousness. Teilhard formalized this understanding of a continuum of divinity in terms of two types of energy, which he called "tangential" and "radial." Tangential energy characterized the mechanistic laws of Newtonian physics and was the dominant force in the realm of scientific exploration. Teilhard called it the energy of "without." Radial energy, on the other hand, was the energy of "within," or the divine spark.

The scientist in Teilhard was not content simply to name the divine spark as radial energy. He also wanted to place it within the context of his larger project—creating a schema for the whole of the evolutionary process. Teilhard further refined his idea of radial energy as a continuum that expressed itself in all aspects of reality. He called the divine spark he saw in inanimate objects "pre-life." In non-self-reflective

8. Teilhard de Chardin, *The Phenomenon of Man,* page 219.

beings, he called it "life." And in humans, he called it "consciousness."[9] The division of the world into the two forces of radial and tangential made sense of the mystical experiences that punctuated Teilhard's life, profound moments that convinced him even the inanimate was infused with the divine.

As Teilhard began to apply his new insight to the world described by science, he noticed that in certain things, such as rocks, the tangential energy was dominant, while the radial energy was barely visible. In other things, such as animals, the radial energy was greater and its effects on the organism were quite noticeable. Teilhard concluded that when tangential energy was stronger, the evolutionary process would best be characterized by the traditional scientific view. Necessity and chance, the laws of scientific evolution, would be the most apt descriptors. But, in those organisms where the radial energy dominated, the forces of life and consciousness would be the primary factors to lead evolution forward.

Teilhard then took his insight a step further. He saw that as the balance of radial energy in any given entity grew larger, it developed naturally in the direction of higher consciousness. Teilhard refined this observation into what he called the "law of complexity-consciousness," which stated, quite simply, that increasing complexity is accompanied by increased consciousness. Teilhard the paleontologist observed that radial energy, the energy of consciousness, had the same granular quality as matter. In other words, within the context of evolutionary time, consciousness, like matter, had the tendency to build itself into more complex arrangements. As this happened, a certain critical mass of con-

---

9. As Teilhard writes in *The Phenomenon of Man* (page 57), "Here, and throughout this book, the term 'consciousness' is taken in its widest sense to indicate every kind of psychism, from the most rudimentary forms of interior perception imaginable to the human phenomenon of reflective thought."

sciousness would be born. When this critical mass was reached, the energy of consciousness, not that of physics and chemistry, would lead the process of evolution forward.

The law of complexity-consciousness went hand-in-hand with a concept Teilhard called "orthogenesis." Orthogenesis was Teilhard's term for the force inherent in the evolutionary process that directs all growth and change toward increased complexity and consciousness. This concept underscored the central kernel of Teilhard's thought—evolution is not a process of blind chance. It is in some very real sense guided. Evolution, in other words, wants to find consciousness. As Teilhard wrote, "evolution would fundamentally be nothing else than the continual growth of this 'psychic' or 'radial' energy, in the course of duration, beneath and within the mechanical energy I called 'tangential.' "[10] For Teilhard, the primary stuff of evolution was not mechanistic or material; rather, it was the inner spark that fires evolutionary process.

Teilhard then identified a "selective mechanism for the play of consciousness"[11]—the nervous system. For Teilhard, evolutionary history was not written only in bones, cranium size, or morphological structure, but in the development of nervous systems. He claimed that when the history of living things is categorized by the evolution of their nervous systems, a natural order emerges. Christian de Duve, a Nobel Laureate in biology, supports Teilhard's theory in his book *Vital Dust*. De Duve argues that once something like a neuron emerges, "neuronal networks of increasing complexity are almost bound to arise. The drive toward larger brains, and, therefore, toward greater consciousness, intelligence, and communication ability dominates the animal limb of the tree of life." The tracing of life through the evolution of the nervous

---

10. Teilhard de Chardin, *The Phenomenon of Man,* page 143.
11. Ibid., page 144.

system was Teilhard's means of examining the objective pathways of consciousness, forming the scientific aspect of his theory.

In terms of the issue of spiritually guided evolution, it is Teilhard's mapping of the interior aspect, of consciousness itself, that is of primary interest. Teilhard wrote, "To write the true natural history of the world, we should need to be able to follow it from *within*. It would thus appear no longer as an interlocking succession of structural types replacing one another, but as an ascension of inner sap spreading out in a forest of consolidated instincts. Right at its base, the living world is constituted by consciousness clothed in flesh and bone. From the biosphere to the species is nothing but an immense ramification of psychism seeking for itself through different forms."[12]

Teilhard posited a highly specific map of this internal evolution that leads through three distinct phases of evolutionary development. The first major phase began with life itself or the emergence of the biosphere from the physiosphere. This phase marked the end of the time when geogenesis, or geological evolution, was the primary axis of evolution. Of course, this development did not mark the end of geological evolution. His essential point was that with the birth of life, the center of gravity of the evolutionary process shifted to the realm of biological evolution, or what Teilhard called "biogenesis."

The second phase of evolution began with the emergence of conscious beings. This huge leap, as Teilhard took pains to point out, was marked by relatively insignificant external changes in factors such as the size and shape of the brain cavity. Nonetheless, on the interior level, the emergence of consciousness has clearly had enormously profound ramifications. With the birth of self-reflective thought, the axis of evolution shifted firmly from the process of biogenesis to the realm of

---

12. Ibid., page 151.

noogenesis, a term Teilhard derived from the Greek *nous*, for "mind."

Teilhard, in his often poetic style, wrote of this evolutionary moment, "A glow ripples outward from the first spark of conscious reflection. The point of ignition grows larger. The fire spreads in ever widening circles till finally the whole planet is covered with incandescence. Only one interpretation, only one name can be found worthy of this grand phenomenon. Much more coherent and just as extensive as any preceding layer, it is really a new layer, the 'thinking layer,' which, since its germination at the end of the Tertiary period, has spread over and above the world of plants and animals. In other words, outside and above the biosphere there is the noosphere."[13] The noosphere represents a stage of evolution characterized by a complex membrane of thought, fueled by human consciousness, enveloping the globe. This distinctly nontraditional evolutionary idea may strike us as odd until we consider the phenomenon of cyberspace, that electronically supported layer of human consciousness that now encircles the globe.

HARDWIRING THE NOOSPHERE

"What Teilhard was saying can be summed up in a few words," says John Perry Barlow, cofounder of the Electronic Frontier Foundation. "The point of all evolution to this stage is to create a collective organism of mind. With cyberspace, we are essentially hardwiring the noosphere."

Cyberspace, the vast web of electronic information encircling the earth through a nervelike constellation of wires, represents the most

---

13. Ibid., page 182.

powerful instantiation of the noosphere to date. Though he died in 1955, Teilhard had a sense that noogenesis would be greatly enhanced by the discovery of electronic communication. He wrote, "What, in fact, do we see happening in the modern paroxysm? It has been stated over and over again. Through the discovery yesterday of the railway, the motor car and the aeroplane, the physical influence of each man, formerly restricted to a few miles, now extends to hundreds of leagues or more. Better still: thanks to the prodigious biological event represented by the discovery of electro-magnetic waves, each individual finds himself henceforth (actively and passively) simultaneously present, over land and sea, in every corner of the earth."[14]

When Teilhard used the terms *actively* and *passively* to describe the ways in which we, the products and the producers of the noosphere, now find ourselves "simultaneously present" over the whole world, he was referring to the twin dimensions of radial and tangential energies. At the level of the noosphere, these two forces play out in the forms of *interiorization* and *organization* within a societal context. "Interiorization" refers to the ability of radial energy, the spiritual dimension, to mutually interpenetrate and combine. In human experience, this interiorization is felt most directly as the synthetic nature of our consciousness. As we move in social groups, our thoughts and ideas tend to be shared and communicated, creating a nontangible, interpenetrating web of consciousness. In the contemporary world, this tendency is ever more marked as we find certain notions permeating the global culture. "Organization" refers to the external ordering of the mechanical and social processes that support noogenesis.

Cyberspace is a powerful expression of both interiorization and

---

14. Ibid., page 240.

organization. The global communications infrastructure of cyberspace, formed by a network of satellites and wires, mainframes, servers, and personal computers, forms its organizational aspect. Its interior aspect is made up of a free flow of consciousness, controlled by no one, that anyone with a connection can plug into. Together, these two aspects make the noosphere tangible to us, drawing us into a world whose primary quality is the constant, ever-changing synthesis of information. One important hallmark of this process is the emergence of a global weltanschauung whose strength and depth, for better or worse, is being geometrically enhanced by the presence of cyberspace. As Teilhard wrote, "The mind is essentially the power of synthesis and organization."[15] Synthesis and organization are also the powers of cyberspace, a realm born of the noosphere and located firmly within it.

Teilhard believed that since its inception, the noosphere had been growing naturally in the direction of greater density and complexity, reflecting and furthering the ongoing growth of consciousness on the planet. Ultimately, he believed, the noosphere would coalesce into "the living unity of a single tissue" containing our collective thoughts and experiences. The final force pushing evolution in this direction is the force of compression. Teilhard argued that the constraints of the physical universe, the built-in material limitations documented by science, have exerted certain boundaries on evolutionary development. If evolution had operated without these constraints, matter would never have concentrated enough to give birth to life. It would instead be spread in a thin, undifferentiated layer across an infinite universe.

Life on earth has been subject to even stricter limitations. The resources of the globe, where life as we know it has evolved, are finite.

---

15. Ibid., page 259.

The spread of humanity across the world, argued Teilhard, further restricted the available resources, concentrating and compressing the human evolutionary process. This concentration and compression serve to enhance the growth in self-reflective consciousness or thought that comprises the noosphere.

Compression, organization, and interiorization—these are the forces of noogenesis. These forces, which began with the Neolithic and continue to exert their pressures in increasing amounts, have resulted in the formation of a highly interdependent, global social structure. As Teilhard wrote, "Peoples and civilizations reached such a degree either of frontier contact or economic interdependence or psychic communion that they could no longer develop save by interpenetration of one another. But it also arises out of the fact that, under the combined influence of machinery and super-heating of thought, we are witnessing a formidable upsurge of unused powers."[16]

With the emergence of thinking humanity, the forces of compression became more pronounced, leading to the "super-heating" of thought, or what we might think of as an increase in the dynamic interchange of ideas. As these forces gathered steam, the power of invention became a dominant factor in the ongoing evolutionary direction of the planet. Prior to the phase of noogenesis, chance and groping led evolution forward. Now invention leads the way. In this context, the machines we create, our technologies, are leading factors in the evolutionary process. That seems clear enough. What is less clear is how our inventions and exchange of ideas will lead toward the unified, spiritually based future that Teilhard envisioned.

We now stand at the cusp of the third phase of evolution, a point where, as Teilhard explained, "we have become conscious of the

---

16. Ibid., page 252.

movement that is carrying us along." We are, in essence, evolution become aware of itself.[17] This realization, which Teilhard called the "illumination," represents that moment when "the consciousness of each of us is evolution looking at itself and reflecting upon itself."[18]

This is a profound moment in history. We find ourselves participating actively in our own evolutionary process. This power carries with it enormous potential pitfalls, particularly when we assume incorrectly that we can influence processes and structures whose complexity far exceeds our ability to understand them. The power of evolution becoming conscious of itself is, in its highest expression, a spiritual understanding marked by paradox, humility, and a constant call to further expand our own consciousness. Teilhard referred to this as the process of personalization, a process that cyberspace could have a unique role in supporting.

CYBERSPACE, SPİRİT, AND THE NOOSPHERE

Teilhard's vision of evolutionary spheres nested within evolutionary spheres—from the physiosphere to the noosphere—represents a series of wholes that are both closed and centered. It follows from this understanding that all the layers in the universe must be centered at a point where all the radii meet. Teilhard called this quasi-mystical point Omega.

Omega is a concentration of pure consciousness and absolute unity, where "all being is synthesized and organized." In more traditional

---

17. As Teilhard acknowledges, this phrase is borrowed from Julian Huxley.

18. Teilhard de Chardin, *The Phenomenon of Man*, page 221.

terms, Omega is God or pure spirit. Spirit, for Teilhard, is both the lure toward which evolution is continually drawn and the ever-present ground from which it springs. Therefore, Omega includes Alpha and all that is in between. As the synthesis of all centers, Omega is a concentration of consciousness that includes all consciousness. In this sense, it is omniscient. Omega is a place of nonduality where the energies of the personal and the impersonal, of religion and science, of subjective and objective, culminate simultaneously in one another.

Central to understanding Teilhard's vision of the role that spirit or Omega plays in the evolutionary process is his concept of personalization. As evolution moves forward, it incorporates greater degrees of consciousness. As we manifest increasing consciousness, we are essentially bringing to earth greater degrees of spirit, which is itself pure consciousness. Therefore, evolution is, in a very real sense, a process of moving closer toward union with spirit.

What is unique about Teilhard's understanding of this movement toward spirit is that it does not require a dissolution of personality. According to Teilhard, as we move closer to spirit, we approach a place of "harmonized complexity"[19] or what he also called the "hyper-personal." As Teilhard wrote, "What is the work of works for man if not to establish, in and by each one of us, an absolutely original centre in which the universe reflects itself in a unique and inimitable way? And those centres are our very selves and personalities. The very centre of our consciousness, deeper than all its radii; that is the essence which Omega, if it is to be truly Omega, must reclaim."[20]

If the motor of evolution, spirit, is in fact a supreme consciousness, Teilhard argued, would it not make sense that it would inspire in us

---

19. Ibid., page 262.
20. Ibid., page 261.

greater consciousness, the ability to personalize or reflect back upon ourselves? He wrote, "It is only in the direction of hyper-reflection, that is to say, hyper-personalization, that thought can extrapolate itself."[21]

If spirit contains all consciousness, then it is vital that each person remain aware of his or her uniqueness even while incorporating ever more spiritual understanding and insight. As Teilhard explained, each person's consciousness actually becomes more acutely aware of itself and thus more clearly distinct the closer it gets to Omega or spirit. But he cautioned us not to confuse what he called "individuality" with "personality."[22] To cultivate one's individuality is to encourage one's separateness, a step that atomizes the universe into falsely independent units. To develop the personality, on the other hand, is to develop that which is most deeply personal, the essence of one's being. "The peak of ourselves, the acme of our originality, is not our individuality but our person; and according to the evolutionary structure of the world, we can only find our person by uniting together. There is no mind without synthesis. The same law holds good from top to bottom. The true ego grows in inverse proportion to 'egoism.' Like Omega which attracts it, the element only becomes personal when it universalizes itself."[23]

Cyberspace can serve to both further and strengthen the centering of the noosphere as well as the accompanying force of personalization. We participate in cyberspace as clear and distinct individuals. The sharing and merging of our thoughts in this experiential realm does not result in a melting of identity. Quite the opposite. Although identity in cyberspace takes on a new fluidity, its presence remains central to the experience of the environment. How we choose to present ourselves

21. Ibid., page 259.
22. Ibid., page 263.
23. Ibid.

matters in cyberspace. At the same time, in cyberspace we cannot rely on any of the conventional means for personal and social location such as physical appearance or prestige. We are wholly reliant on our inner resources when we participate in this realm.

Our experiences in cyberspace are still relatively new and unformed. We are like children learning to swim. Part of our learning curve is recognizing how to deal with the dark side of cyberspace while we navigate the next turn of the evolutionary spiral. This dark side is deeply connected with a neurotic expression of ego needs. There are countless examples of people becoming addicted to cyberspace, spending hundreds of hours a month developing rather shallow relationships on-line, avoiding all connection to others in the real world. This is not evolutionary but a clear devolution, an escape into a lesser and more fearful part of the self. Cyberspace is a technology of connection, a space where love can manifest itself in many forms. Of course, at the same time as it is breeding connection, it can also breed separation and isolation. As in the larger process of spiritual evolution, the dark and the light coexist in a constant, dialectical tension that serves to move the entire process forward.

John Perry Barlow, who has more experience in this new realm than most, tells a pair of stories that illustrate this point. Several years ago, Barlow met and fell in love with a beautiful and talented woman with whom he was planning to spend the rest of his life. They were together for only a year before she died quite suddenly. He was devastated. After her death, he wrote a brief eulogy, which he then sent electronically to a handful of friends. Some of these friends reproduced it, and, as messages have a tendency to do in cyberspace, it continued to reproduce. In a short period of time, Barlow received "over a megabyte of e-mail from all over the planet from people I didn't know, saying extraordinary things, truly extraordinary. These people were demonstrating love of a very pure sort. We didn't know each other, we are never going to meet, but there was something in my story that touched them. It engaged in the real meat of what I think is human experience and intimacy. It was enormously inspirational to me."

Some time later, he experienced the flip side of cyberspace's connective abilities, what he refers to as the "secret traps." He undertook a love affair on the Net that was "almost entirely virtual due to the fact that it was illicit. She and I could not communicate at all, we couldn't even talk on the phone because she was working with her husband and was never more than eight feet away from him. It was incredibly intense. One hundred fifty thousand words of e-mail in close to six months. What I started to realize, however, was that every time I would see her, she would be even further away. What I realized was that we were each taking the spaces between the words and filling them with our own narcissistic projections of ourselves. It was far more separating than anything like that I've done before. Now I know, so I am aware of that pitfall. But there are millions more that I haven't discovered yet."

Teilhard wrote, "Something will explode if we persist in trying to squeeze into our old tumble-down huts the material and spiritual forces that are henceforward on the scale of the world." He was right about this. The powers that are unleashed by our new technologies, by the increasing concentration of our social and economic systems, by the ongoing development of the noosphere itself, are of a new order. It should come as no great surprise that we have a strong tendency to fall back on inherited means for dealing with these powers, but, as history has shown, these means often deliver us into places of isolation, not connection. For example, it can be cogently argued that the return to violent, nationalistic values evidenced in places like Bosnia is a reaction against the dominance of the emerging global culture enabled by computer technology.

The evolution of humanity is littered with failed attempts at union. In fact, many of the most powerful attempts have led to totalitarian solutions and societies that leave little room for the forces of noogenesis. What is missing in many of these attempts is the understanding that a material and mechanistic approach has a strong tendency to lead to a material and mechanistic solution. In other words, if we approach the issue from the outside, ignoring the forces of consciousness and love, there will be little chance for consciousness and love to be part of the solution. This may seem obvious, but in fact, attempts to find solutions to human social issues are infused with this approach. We live in a time when we believe that science alone is adequate. But science without soul cannot lead to deep connection. As we pursue the material and the quantifiable, we become externally identified and, by extension, greatly reduce our ability to join center to center with others. We can see this approach in abundance in the world around us. In our struggle to find meaning in one of the most powerful consumer cultures ever to erupt on the planet, we fill our lives with things, and our isolation and loneliness only grow.

The process of interpersonal synthesis is fundamental to the movement toward a more spiritual experience of cyberspace. In this context, it is imperative that we take a closer look at the power of love. As Teilhard warned us, not every kind of union will achieve personalization. What is required is the achievement of a "synthesis of centres"—we must make contact from deep within ourselves. Teilhard wrote, "Amongst the various forms of psychic inter-activity animating the noosphere, the energies we must identify, harness and develop before all others are those of an 'intercentric' nature, if we want to give effective help to the progress of evolution in ourselves."[24] This joining of center

---

24. Ibid., page 261.

to center can be achieved only through love. Love, when all is said and done, is the fundamental force of connection that exists in Omega. According to Teilhard, consciousness *is* love, that which connects and synthesizes, the energy that holds the universe together from the smallest quantum event up to the incandescence of the noosphere itself. He wrote that "love alone is capable of uniting human living beings in such a way as to complete or fulfill them, for it alone takes them and joins them by what is deepest in themselves."[25]

Teilhard believed that love is the force that personalizes by totalizing. "A universal love is not only psychologically possible; it is the only complete and final way in which we are able to love."[26] In the form of Omega or spirit, this love is both universal and personal, both in the future and in the supremely present in any given moment. Thus, evolution is a process of both collective movement and individual participation. It is both within our reach and beyond our control. Like Teilhard, we move forward both as scientists seeking to discover, interpret, and participate in an ongoing process of evolution, and as people of faith who watch the cycles of birth and death with the awestruck conviction that at any given moment, spirit is present and all is as it should be.

In understanding Omega or spirit, it is important to note that in Teilhard's view, Omega was the absolute end point of evolution. Whether or not he was right about the ultimate destination of the evolutionary process is beyond our ability to know. What we do know, however, is that the energy of Omega, of spirit, is present and available to us right now, as the ground of evolution. Spirit is that which enables us to access the forces of noogenesis and continue to build architectures for love. Environments such as cyberspace, so clearly an expression of

---

25. Ibid., page 265.
26. Ibid., page 267.

the noosphere, can play a particularly resonant role with our current phase of evolution—of evolution become conscious of itself. The levels of information and global connectivity available through cyberspace can enhance each of our experiences of "harmonized complexity," of being both fully free to express our most unique selves while participating in a synthetic, global context.

If we can overcome the forces of repulsion that lead to isolation and allow ourselves to embrace the trajectory of noogenesis, we will then be on the road to the ultimate expression of the noosphere. As the noosphere further concentrates and centers, through the participation of each of us, the earth does more than find a new evolutionary layer. It finds its soul. The process of noogenesis is ultimately a movement toward the expression of the spirit of the earth through consciousness. The essential lesson of this expression for us at this juncture in history is that "union differentiates." In order for the totality of the earth to express its deepest spiritual nature, we must learn to come together in our uniqueness, to embrace and express the treasure that is each of our souls. Cyberspace, as it extends our abilities to unify and differentiate, may have a powerful hand in this process.

As Bishop Gaillot so astutely recognized, what is important is not to claim physical power in a physical place but to establish communities of faith. This is the real food of the soul and spirit in each of us. By enabling experiments such as Gaillot's in Partenia, cyberspace acts to create new forms of faith communities that exist on a global level and yet are based on deep, personal interactions. At the same time, as Gaillot points out, although these communities exist primarily in the virtual, they need not be abstracted from the needs of the larger societies in which they are embedded.

It is one of cyberspace's earliest and most profound lessons that the more we join together across national and international boundaries, interacting and exchanging experiences with people we may never meet in the flesh, we are not melting into an undifferentiated mass. Cyberspace is not a place of dissolution; it is a place that shows us that we can be distinct and yet not atomized, joined together through our common humanity and sense of self. In this way, cyberspace has the potential to help us embrace the basic truth that as we become more fully individuated, we can find the inner resources we need to create strong and healthy communities. If cyberspace can aid in this progression, it will truly be an important way station on our journey toward greater spiritual evolution.

(4)

NETS OF SILICON, WEBS OF FLESH

In the Hindu tradition, the god Indra was said to possess a magnificent fishing net that encircled the entire universe. An exquisite jewel rested at each juncture in the net where two ropes crossed. These jewels had a very special quality. Each one in the seemingly infinite net reflected every other jewel simultaneously. Therefore, one could look into any one jewel and see within it the whole of the universe. This lovely myth captures one of the great theological truths held by many of the world's religious traditions. Divinity is, by definition, a continuous, unbroken force. Once one becomes aware of the smallest spark of divinity, one touches the whole. Therefore, each small piece of the universe serves as a doorway to the entirety of the divine. Meditating on the proverbial grain of sand can lead one to the sacred truth of the entire universe.

Indra's net serves as a potent metaphor for cyberspace. This nascent digital world contains a remarkable structural similarity to the god Indra's divine net. From any node on the Internet, one can reach all the other nodes or jewels that are present. All of cyberspace can be accessed from any given part. The only requirement is that one be linked in. Cyberspace is a continuous realm of creative experience woven into a vast, relational, dynamically linked whole. By extension, when we touch the divine creative experience as it manifests in cyberspace, we are touching the same divine force that permeates the entire universe. Divine creativity serves as the through-line connecting the bioelectronic ecosystem of cyberspace with the larger ecosystem we call the universe.

As an ecosystem, cyberspace shares certain structural qualities with the larger sacred ecosystem that we think of as reality. Within this structure, cyberspace fulfills a very specific and special role. Cyberspace directly affects the evolution of consciousness, that mysterious and dynamic realm of spiritual unfolding that we humans actively participate in. Taking a closer look at the specific qualities of cyberspace's sacred ecology helps us to further clarify our role in the ongoing spiritual evolution of the universe.

Essentially a medium for human communication, cyberspace is deeply embedded in and beholden to human consciousness. Human consciousness gave birth to cyberspace and continues to fuel its ongoing unfolding. This understanding helps us to locate cyberspace within the many layers of reality that make up the universe. While cyberspace has links into the physical, through hardware, and the biological, through our bodies, its most active and potent aspects are to be found at the level of mind or consciousness. Cyberspace's center of gravity is located squarely in the noosphere.

The noosphere extends from, but is not reducible to, the biosphere, or the realm of life. The biosphere, in turn, extends from but is not reducible to the physiosphere, or the material world. For example, conscious human experience is embedded in human bodies. Even so, an examination of our bodies cannot explain the mystery of consciousness.

Neurons and electrochemical signals in the brain do not make sense of why we have subjective experience, or why this subjective experience is necessary.[1] However, human consciousness cannot exist without our biological selves, our bios. In the same vein, our bodies are utterly dependent on the intricate web of biological and physical relationships that constitute the larger ecosystem we think of as the earth. All of these complex layers of interdependence constitute the evolving reality that we perceive around us.

When one extracts one aspect of the whole and analyzes it independently of the world in which it is embedded, a very limited understanding emerges. In some cases, as ecological philosophy would argue, serious errors arise from such analysis in a vacuum. One can take apart an ecosystem and study just one species, a common practice among many scientists, but the resulting information produces a very specific and limited understanding. In order to fully understand any given species, one must analyze the world in which it lives, eats, reproduces, and dies. This is precisely the message of ecological science—things must be understood in the larger context of the systems in which they are embedded.

The ecological message points to the fundamental truth that everything is connected to everything else in an endlessly nested system. One way of beginning to tease apart and understand this massively complex ecological web is to start with the obvious—everything that exists is both a whole unto itself and part of the larger system in which it is embedded. Arthur Koestler coined a term for this concept, *holon*, which means something is both a whole and a part, or a whole/part. When one begins to see that the world is made up of an infinite nesting

---

1. For a much more extensive discussion of this issue, see David Chalmers, *The Conscious Mind*.

of holons, a much more sophisticated view of reality begins to emerge.

The primary advantage of Koestler's concept is that it leaves room for the processes that underlie the universe to take their rightful place. The holon-based view enables us to grasp the essential nature of the universe as an endless dynamic of wholes and processes melting into wholes and processes. As Whitehead's metaphysics so clearly points out, the great All of the universe is composed of infinite events that flow into infinite new events. Holons, like Whitehead's occasions of experience, serve as a doorway into both the deeper structure of cyberspace and the larger space of reality from which it is born.

Ken Wilber, a philosopher who has spent many years articulating a complex, holon-based worldview, tells an old joke that illustrates the basic concept. Long ago, a king went to a wise person and asked, "How is it that the earth doesn't fall down?" The wise person answered, "The earth is resting on a lion." The king then asked, "What then is the lion resting on?" "The lion is resting on an elephant." "What is the elephant resting on?" "The elephant is resting on a turtle." "What then is the . . ." "You can stop right there, your majesty. It's turtles all the way down."[2]

Turtles all the way down, and by extension, all the way up. Holons all the way down and all the way up. The underlying truth of this joke is that in the universe around us, there are no parts and there are no wholes. Only whole/parts or holons. At the subatomic level, holons melt into holons in an infinite dance of particles and waves. At the universal level, the whole of the universe in each moment becomes a part of the universe in the very next moment. What we think of as wholes or parts, or elephants and turtles, become waves of ongoing unfolding in the larger process of evolution.

---

2. Ken Wilber, *Sex, Ecology, Spirituality*, page 35.

CYBERSPACE'S SACRED ECOLOGY: HOLONS AND HOLOARCHY

Cyberspace forms a unique and startlingly new holon. It, in turn, is composed of a myriad of smaller holons. Understanding both the holon of cyberspace as well as the holons that make it up will shed light on its role in the evolutionary process.

All holons display certain characteristics in the evolutionary dance. Wilber has taken care throughout his many books to develop a rigorous and insightful structure that points out a handful of central qualities. Wilber's work is remarkably coherent with both Whitehead's metaphysics and Teilhard de Chardin's philosophy, so I won't belabor the points that are redundant. However, a quick outline of what Wilber refers to as the basic tenets of holons will help in our understanding of the evolutionary role of cyberspace.

Wilber begins with the contention that there is nothing in the world that is not a holon. From atoms, cells, and symbols to ideas and strings of computer code, everything is a holon, or both a whole unto itself and a part of something else. Each of these holons displays four fundamental features—self-preservation, self-adaptation, self-transcendence, and self-dissolution. The first characteristic of a holon, self-preservation, or what Wilber calls "agency," refers to a holon's ability to maintain an autonomous and coherent pattern of expression. This is its "wholeness" aspect, or what we might think of as its objective, externally observable qualities. For example, the holon of an e-mail message will contain certain words, have a beginning and an end, and exist within a certain software format. But, as the second feature, self-adaptation, points out, an e-mail message also exists within a specific context, cyberspace. In this context, it must be able to adapt to the demands of its environment in order to continue to exist. In other words, the packet of symbols and electricity that compose the e-mail message must move successfully through a complex series of transformations in order to go from my computer to yours. In fact, the average e-mail message undergoes at least nine distinct transformations or permutations as it moves from point to point through cyberspace. Wilber refers to self-adaptation as "communion."

Self-preservation and self-adaptation, or agency and communion, represent the two opposing pulls on any holon—wholeness and partness. Agency represents wholeness, while communion refers to the partness. Wilber points out that imbalances between these two forces are what create pathology in any given holon. In the most extreme case, if either force drops out of the picture altogether, the holon itself will cease to exist.

The next pair of fundamental features Wilber isolates are self-transcendence and self-dissolution. Self-transcendence is Whitehead's divine creativity, no more, no less. This feature refers to the inherent evolutionary ability of a holon to display novelty and creative transformation, to move beyond what it is and manifest something utterly new. Self-transcendence, as we have already noted, is a primary motor of the evolutionary process. When a holon transcends itself, it reaches a new level of being and will therefore express new types of agency and communion. Self-dissolution refers to the opposite pull, or the ability of a holon to dissolve or come apart. According to Wilber, this dissolution will tend to occur in the same order in which a holon was built up. Taken together, the four forces of agency, communion, creativity, and dissolution form the basic pulls that any holon must continually contend with.

All holons exist within a larger pattern of reality. But this reality is organized in a special way in order to accommodate them. Holons exist in a *holoarchy*, a structural paradigm that has much in common with the image of Indra's net and with cyberspace itself. A holoarchy is a hierarchically arranged system that runs from the lowest rung, the physiosphere, up through the biosphere to the noosphere and beyond that to the realm of transcendent spirit. A holoarchy is *not* a hierarchy. Hierarchies are flat and their order implies a qualitative difference between levels; i.e., the higher levels are better than the lower levels. In contrast, a holoarchic view incorporates the distinct levels that exist in the world around us as an ordering device. But, at the same time, because holoarchies are made up of holons and not discrete objects, each level of the holoarchy is utterly dependent on and linked to every other level. In a holoarchy, each holon is intrinsically valuable. In other words, every holon has worth by definition of its very existence.

Within a holoarchy, holons emerge holoarchically. This means that each new holon both transcends but *includes* the holons that precede it. In doing so, the evolutionary process of self-transcendence consistently weaves reality into a tighter and more complex web. As Wilber writes, each holon "*preserves* the previous holons themselves but *negates* their separateness or isolatedness or aloneness. It preserves their being but negates their partiality or exclusiveness."[3]

Cyberspace embodies the holoarchic paradigm. In order to understand how this is true, we must first understand some of the primary holons that constitute the world of cyberspace. We begin with the holon of the machine itself, the rigidly engineered hardware that we think of as a computer. Add to this the many levels of software that bring it alive. Within the software, smaller holons can be found, ranging from basic machine code, the strings of 0s and 1s that interact directly with the hardware, to increasingly complex algorithms that

---

3. Ibid., page 51.

dictate the inner workings of the program. Rising up the chain of complexity, we find that the next holon takes the form of human/computer interfaces, high-level programming code that encompasses everything from virtual reality and graphics-based applications to the more familiar pull-down menus and text-based interfaces that many of us use every day. The holons of hardware and software can then be understood as joining with the world of human agency to form the complex holon of cyberspace. The holon of cyberspace not only includes individual experience but manifests at the social and cultural levels.

In cyberspace, as in real space, each higher level emerges from and is dependent on the lower levels. As Wilber points out, the lower holons set the possibilities for the higher, while the higher set the probabilities for the lower. In other words, the limitations of the hardware, such as memory capacity and processor speed, directly implicate the limitations of the software. At the same time, the higher levels of human consciousness impose patterns on the lower levels of software and hardware that order them in certain ways. Without the ordering abilities of the higher levels, the lower levels would be more chaotic. The higher levels weave together and strengthen the lower levels.

One can see the active nature of holoarchies clearly in the historical development of cyberspace. As more and more people come on-line, and more sophisticated techniques for being in cyberspace are born, the whole of the Net becomes increasingly ordered and strengthened.[4] In the early days of cyberspace—when it was composed of relatively

---

4. This is a somewhat controversial statement in light of the many doomsday predictions about overloading the Net and the inevitability of connection crash, a state that occurs when the balance of connections in a system reaches the overload point. It is my contention, however, that new developments will continue to be produced that will avoid any catastrophic breakdown of the system. At the very least, there are excellent financial incentives for companies and individuals to create products that circumvent the breakdown of the Net. I believe there are also larger, evolutionary reasons to trust that this potent new realm will find a way to continue to grow and strengthen.

uncomplicated, text-based systems running along dedicated data lines—the Net was simpler, slower, and laughably crude. The traditional explanation for this would be that it was limited by the available technology. But, according to Wilber's model, the higher holons, in this case human demand and use, were also more limited. As more people became aware of the Net and started to use it, exerting a pull from above, new hardware emerged to support new applications. The lower holons set the possibilities for the higher while the higher set the probabilities for the lower. In other words, the ongoing development of cyberspace is a multidirectional pull from higher to lower and from lower to higher. Actually, this quality of growing and ordering from use applies throughout the holoarchy of the universe. It is just more acutely palpable at the level of the noosphere. As the noosphere grows and becomes more strongly woven together it exerts new probabilities for the further evolution of the biosphere and the physiosphere. All is woven together in a vastly complex, dynamic whole.

The energies and influences within any holoarchy move not only up and down but from side to side. Recall Indra's net: Any jewel reflects all the other jewels. This is the essence of the holographic or holoarchic paradigm. Cyberspace may be the first experiential environment that so clearly embodies this truth. Information in cyberspace moves about in a radically holoarchic fashion. Through the World Wide Web, for example, one can navigate cyberspace in any direction one chooses. The structure of the space does not require one to move in a linear fashion. There is a constant exchange of information both between lower and higher holons and between holons at the same level. All of this complex activity is utterly interdependent and coevolving.

This brings us to the final set of points about holons. If one gets rid of any given holon, all the holons above it will cease to exist, but those below it will be unaffected. In other words, if one gets rid of machine code, no further software will run. But if one gets rid of the human/computer interface, the machine code and the rest of the programming instructions will run uninterrupted. An important extension of this idea is that as one moves up through the holoarchy, one finds that each successive level includes less span and greater depth. Span refers to the sheer number of holons involved. For example, there are infinitely more 0s and 1s in machine code than there are programming-instruction sets that run the human/computer interface. But, at the same time, the programming instructions have much greater depth or complexity than machine code. Wilber then adds the important corollary that *"the greater the depth of a holon, the greater its degree of consciousness. The spectrum of evolution is a spectrum of consciousness. And one can perhaps begin to see that a spiritual dimension is built into the very fabric, the very depth of the Kosmos."*[5] This crucial point will become clear as the story of cyberspace and holons continues to unfold.

İNDRA'S NET: A SOCİAL HOLON

Wilber divides the world into individual holons and social holons. Both types exhibit the characteristics outlined above, but social holons are more complex than individual holons. Social holons are a special collection of holons that act as a consistent whole and can be characterized almost as a single entity. In other words, social holons display an unusual level of coherence, so it is confusing as to whether they should be thought of as individual holons or a collection of smaller ones. In some cases, social holons are so tightly unified that they appear to be

5. Ken Wilber, *Sex, Ecology, Spirituality*, page 57.

almost "superorganisms."[6] Wilber uses the example of an ant colony to illustrate the phenomenon of a social holon.

Cyberspace as a totality forms a new type of social holon. When seen from this perspective, it makes sense that to characterize the fundamental nature of cyberspace is difficult. It clearly consists of the input of millions of individuals, each generating thousands of individual holons—ideas and feelings that contain symbols (language), which in turn contain software code that is made up of algorithms that can be reduced to electrical packets that traverse complex hardware configurations. On the other hand, cyberspace as a system seems to be more than a myriad of individual holons flashing around in time and space. It is also a coherent environment, a social holon that we can point to and experience. As such, it follows the basic rules of all holons, but with an additional aspect that becomes clear from examining the schematic grid Wilber has constructed for mapping holons.

In this grid, Wilber has outlined four distinct quadrants. The upper left and right refer to the worlds of individual holons, while the lower left and right map the social holons. Keep in mind, of course, that owing to the very nature of holons, each one exists in all four realms. But for the moment, envisioning the grid will help simplify the whole and locate cyberspace within the evolutionary holoarchy of the universe.

Following in the footsteps of Whitehead and Teilhard de Chardin as well as others, Wilber postulates that every holon includes both a within and a without, or an interior and an exterior facet. The exterior is the holon's form, the aspect that can be objectively observed. The interior is the energy of consciousness, Teilhard's "tangential energy," Whitehead's "experience." For Wilber, all holons have an interiority,

---

6. Ibid., page 65.

which he characterizes as depth. Of course, an atom has much less depth than a cell or an idea and therefore less observable consciousness. The amount of consciousness in any holon is relative to its place in the holoarchy. As one moves up through the holoarchy, one encounters holons of greater depth, complexity, and consciousness. This is Teilhard's law of complexity-consciousness and Wilber's contention that as one ascends the holoarchy, one finds greater depth (consciousness) and less span.

Individual holons have a within that begins at the lowest levels with experience, in the sense that Whitehead used the term. The next stage is sensation, which can be found in organisms with neurons. The interior aspect then appears as emotions in animals with limbic systems, symbols in animals with simple neocortexes, and concepts in the complex neocortexes of humans. Within individual humans, another series of interior experiences can be mapped based on developmental psychology and spiritual evolution. For our purposes, however, we will begin by examining the portion of Wilber's work that maps the interior and exterior of social holons, or what he calls the cultural and social aspects.

First, we will examine cyberspace from its exterior location. Borrowing from the work of Alastair Taylor, Wilber erects a holoarchy of the exterior aspects of social holons. This holoarchy begins with kinship systems and moves up through villages, empires, and nation-states toward planetary systems. Our current location in this scheme is at the level of the nation-state, the level that gave birth to democracy. This social level emerged on the heels of the machine age, a time characterized by Newtonian science, machine technology, and the mechanical transmission of information. To drastically simplify a very complex story of social emergence, democracy can be seen as coevolutionary with technological developments that encouraged personal freedom on many levels. With the introduction of the machine, for the first time in human history, people were granted some real autonomy from the physically laborious processes of keeping life going. In a complex dialectical process, the fruits of the machine coevolved with the birth of democratic ideas, most strongly in those nations where mechanical progress was unfolding rapidly.

Cyberspace, or the electronic transmission of information, was born of the realm of Einsteinian science. Although still in its early stages, cyberspace appears to be coevolving with a more global worldview, one that transcends the limitations of the democratic nation-state. Cyberspace is the primary technology that undergirds a more ecumenical, international, and automated world. In Wilber's scheme, cyberspace is located in the transitional phase between democratic nation-states and a planetary system of federated states and interstate organizations. In other words, cyberspace exists on the cusp of a planetary social structure. In fact, according to Taylor's outline, just as the machine age was the technological precursor for democracy, cyberspace could serve as the technological precursor for planetary political organizations or world government.

This idea has been offered before. Many cyber visionaries have heralded cyberspace as the answer to our political and social woes, pointing to its innate democratic and ecumenical features. Cyberspace, for those lucky enough to be on-line, is the great equalizer. My Web page can pack as much punch as IBM's. I can have the same say as the president. Cyberspace is a relatively level playing field, one where the traditional prejudices about how I look, what I wear, and what type of car I drive hold no sway. Some people predict that this new social space will revitalize the democratic system, making it a more participatory and truly grass-roots experience. Cyberspace is clearly working to break down national boundaries with unprecedented speed. When we look out our virtual windows, the neighborhood we see is global, not local. To date, however, Marshall McLuhan's vision of the global village has manifested more in the form of a global bank. The worldwide communications systems of cyberspace work primarily to serve the economic needs of first-world countries. Our economies, long globally interdependent, have become ever more blind to national boundaries thanks to the rapid technological transfer of money and information. Large corporate interests are indeed exercising planetary vision, but this development has many negative side effects. Global marketing and media are blurring cultural and local specificity, creating a homogenized world based on the lowest common denominator of economic advantage. The overall picture is far from rosy.

The danger inherent in the novel social holon of cyberspace is the same danger that any emerging holon presents. If it is not adequately understood that the new form *contains* and *integrates* all the previous forms, the holoarchy is weakened, not strengthened. As we struggle to integrate the new social holon of cyberspace, we stand in real danger of replicating an often-repeated mistake. Instead of genuine integration that respectfully includes the many other holons that have led to this point, we may well fall into the trap of repression. As Wilber writes, "Instead of transcendence, repression; instead of differentiation, dissociation; instead of depth, disease. Because of the very nature of evolution, that type of dissociation can occur at any and all stages of growth and development. The noosphere is not privileged or unique in this regard. It is simply more alarming because of its global dimensions."[7]

Wilber outlines three steps that ideally occur in the healthy inte-

---

7. Ibid., page 104.

gration of a new holon. The first is "fusion/identification." In terms of social integration of cyberspace, much of our culture still stands on the first rungs of this step. As was pointed out in chapter 1, we are all too ready to accept the computational paradigm as *the* new way of viewing the world. In the process of fusing with computers, we unconsciously reduce the world to this powerful and yet limited paradigm. We identify ourselves as comparable to computers and conclude that the secrets of the world will be rendered comprehensible through computation alone. We even posit that the whole of the universe can be replicated in a computer if we can only find the right digital pattern. In fact, there are those who argue that the world we live in is nothing more than a vast computer simulation, running on that big, transcendent computer in the sky that in earlier eras was referred to as God. These are all potent examples of the first stage of fusion/identification.

The second stage, which we are now beginning to see faint glimmers of, is "differentiation/transcendence." The phase may be seen in its earliest incarnation as taking the form of a backlash against computation. How are we *not* like computers? What is special about us? While an important antithesis to the fusion stage, this stage also contains its hidden dangers. One of the most common is the neo-Luddite response that calls for us to go back to an earlier, romanticized period when we didn't have to cope with the alienation and cultural, social, and economic dislocations that cyberspace appears to be spawning. While this may seem attractive, it is entirely impractical as well as regressive. There is no way to go backward. We cannot return to the garden, any more than we can turn off all the computers in the world. Even if we could, we would be very different people facing the pristine world of nature, people more likely than not to become restless and dissatisfied with such unmediated pleasures. Forward is the only realistic and responsible path open to us. This leads to the final step, "integration/inclusion," a step that is more difficult to take than it may at first seem.

The process of fully integrating cyberspace in a healthy manner will require enormous consciousness from each of us. This is the great evolutionary test. At each new rung, the task of healthy integration becomes more complex and requires greater social, personal, and spiritual awareness. In order to truly integrate the local, the personal, the body, the family, and the clan into the great planetary, ecumenical potential offered by cyberspace, we need to find where each of these aspects exists within ourselves. Once we have identified these locations, we can begin to make a conscious effort to integrate them within ourselves and the communities in which we live. As Teilhard de Chardin pointed out, in one of the great spiritual paradoxes, the more we come together into a global whole, the more fully realized each of us will become individually. These two processes, which at first blush appear contradictory, move hand in hand. A healthy planetary consciousness inclusive of cyberspace will require that each of us struggle to integrate the various pieces within him- or herself.

We can fall down at any point along the way. We can get stuck in the mode of fusion, we can repress instead of transcend, we can deny instead of include. Any of these responses to cyberspace can lead to deep dissociation and disease. This does not mean the world will stop, simply that it will continue to limp along in a half-formed way, sickly and out of kilter. It is our response to cyberspace that will in large part determine its future role on the planet.

We are still in the very early phases of coming to terms with cyberspace, and it is too soon to tell whether we are on the path toward repression, dissociation, and disease, or transcendence, differentiation, and depth. If we are to the achieve the latter, it seems clear that at the very least we need to hold as a clear intention the goal of integrating and carrying forward the previous levels of experience. In other words, we cannot privilege the global at the expense of the local, the disembodied in favor of the embodied, or the technological in favor of the organic. We exist in a holoarchic system with cyberspace, our families, our bodies, the trees, the waves, and the stars. An embrace large enough to include all of this will stretch us, push us, ask us to transcend our former worldviews and limitations. In entering a process of healthy and conscious integration with cyberspace, we will evolve. The very essence of the universe asks no less of us.

INFINITE RATIONAL POSSIBILITY: CYBERSPACE'S INNER DIMENSION

In our quest for integration, it is imperative that we seek to understand not only the social location and external form that cyberspace takes in the noosphere but also its internal meaning. It is the interiority that is most often shielded from view and least discussed. Wilber calls this realm the "interior/social" or cultural realm.

The evolutionary movement inherent in the interior aspect of Wilber's chart follows a three-phase process with a new twist. Self-transcendence in the realm of consciousness translates as self-development. In other words, echoing Teilhard, Wilber contends that as one moves up through the realms of conscious awareness, one manifests more and more consciousness in one's life. As one travels into the inner world of consciousness, one is also moving into the realm of spirit. Spirit rules our interior world, the place of creativity, self-transcendence, and conscious awareness. Therefore, as we go within, we gain the possibility of transcending the limited awareness of rational thinking and can begin to embrace the larger, interconnected nature of reality. Interior consciousness forms the bridge beyond the rational to the transrational or transpersonal domains. These domains are realms of awareness broad enough to enfold the sacred truth that divine spirit is woven throughout all that is. Wilber's simple formula for this process is "going within = going beyond = greater embrace."[8]

The way in which this process works itself out in individuals is quite interesting. Wilber contends that the more interior a person becomes, the less egocentric he or she will be. This seems counterintuitive for many of us. We tend to believe that if we go inside, we will become more, not less, self-absorbed. But in reality, moving inward is the key to becoming aware of the function and structure of the ego. It is only through this awareness that we can gain the insight we need to move beyond the rigid hold it has on many of us. As Wilber writes, "The more one can go *within*, or the more one can introspect and reflect on one's self, then the more detached from that self one can become, the more one can rise above that self's limited perspective, and so the less narcissistic or less egocentric one becomes."[9]

This process of going within/going beyond unfolds in increasing depth as one moves up through the rungs of development. At the present time, the interior location of the leading intellectual edge of our culture is at the level of "formal operational" (formop), a stage Wilber borrows from the work of Jean Piaget. Formop represents the highest stage of rational development. As such, it incorporates all the earlier stages of reason, emotion, and sensation and also begins to show traces

---

8. Ibid., page 254.

9. Ibid., page 256.

of the next stage to come. If we look more closely at formop, we see that cyberspace is the perfect manifestation of this stage of conscious development.

Formop is characterized by the ability to transcend the rules of thought themselves. What this means is that reason, at this level, becomes "*a space of possibilities,* possibilities not tied to the obvious, the given, the mundane, the profane."[10] This is the realm of Plato's ideal forms. At the level of formop, one becomes aware of potential worlds and universes that can be seen only by the mind's eye. The world of concrete, material manifestation continues to exert a pull, but with formop, a more transcendent sense of reason comes into play.

A highly relational understanding of the world accompanies the infinite space of possibility that formop ushers in. Here one finds the ability to rise above the apparently discrete and separate nature of the concrete world and understand its interpenetrating aspect. Wilber writes that this realm is "a relationship of mutual interaction and mutual interpenetration, where wholes and parts, while remaining perfectly discrete and intact, are also seen to be what they are by virtue of their relationship to each other."[11] A corollary of this awareness is the understanding that things are relative to one another. The combination of a relative and a relational understanding can lead to the beginnings of a nonanthropocentric worldview; humans become simply another piece in the great web of life. A multicultural and universal perspective also begins to be felt, as people become aware of the relative aspects of the many cultures and races that inhabit the planet.

Formop is also a deeply introspective phase. When the external norms and rules of culture are stripped away by a relativistic perspec-

---

10. Ibid., page 231.
11. Ibid., page 233.

tive, one finds oneself having to form one's own identity independently. The major question of the formop stage is, "Who am I?" Self-esteem needs and identity crises become paramount. And, as Wilber summarizes, "All of this, all of it, comes from being able to see the possibilities of *what might be,* possibilities seen only with the mind's eye, possibilities that point toward worlds not yet in existence and worlds not yet really seen, the great, great doorway to the invisible and beyond."[12]

Cyberspace perfectly embodies this phase, the highest of the rational realms. Like the formop sensibility, cyberspace is a realm of pure possibility, rendered comprehensible through the lens of rational, mathematical forms. It is a world seen by the mind's eye that relies on and includes the realms of emotion and sensation. Cyberspace is relational to its very core, from the ways in which the software and hardware interact and are structured to its social and cultural implications. Perhaps most important, the very nature of cyberspace demands that as we experience it, we access the formop aspects of our own rationality. Cyberspace pushes us inward, into our own space of pure possibility. If this inward movement is utilized correctly, in the service of personal growth and conscious awareness, cyberspace may help us develop the tools necessary for moving to the next stage of spiritual evolution.

TOWARD VISION-LOGIC AND PLANETARY CONSCIOUSNESS

Every holon naturally seeks to transcend itself, reaching to the next level of development. The social holon of cyberspace is no exception.

---

12. Ibid., page 235.

We coevolve with cyberspace as both we and it seek the next steps along the evolutionary path. In concert with cyberspace, we stand at the cusp of the highest expression of rationality, the noosphere, peering into the next level of the theosphere, the realm of the truly transpersonal stages of awareness. The next rung on the journey, the first of the transpersonal stages identified by Wilber, is the realm of vision-logic or "network-logic."

Vision-logic, characterized by a synthetic rationality that apprehends truth as a whole, requires the ability to go within and move beyond reason itself, to see it as simply another aspect of our personal and universal development. To see past reason while not rejecting it requires that we stand in a space of consciousness larger than rationality itself. It is like the fish leaping from the water, looking down and seeing for the first time the world in which it was immersed and understanding that although the water is fundamental to its very being, it does not constitute the whole of the universe. In this way, the stage of vision-logic or synthetic thinking represents the first phase of transrational and transpersonal understanding. With vision-logic, we leap beyond the limitations of the rational ego, integrating the objective world of agency with the subjective world of communion within the framework of a harmoniously realized physiosphere, biosphere, and noosphere.

In leading the way beyond reason, vision-logic begins to introduce to us the mysteries of the transpersonal. Transpersonal consciousness can be both deeply liberating and enormously unsettling. As Wilber points out, on the first rungs of transpersonal understanding, in the neither fully here nor fully there world of vision-logic, a certain dread and fear sets in. When the foundation of pure reason, with its ability to neatly slot the world into tidy boxes, slides slowly out of reach, one is left with a sense of the pure arbitrariness of the structures one has relied on. This is in many ways the core of the postmodern dilemma. As Wilber writes, "When I authentically see my life, I see its ending, I see its death; and I see that my 'other selves,' my ego, my personae, were all sustained by inauthenticity, by an *avoidance* of the awareness of a lonely death."[13]

The dark side of vision-logic manifests as this sense of existential malaise. It is all too easy to get stuck there, madly building defenses against the fear that if one moves on, all will fall apart. This often causes a repression of the earlier states, the physiosphere and the biosphere, and one digs one's heels firmly into the realm of reason, holding on for dear life. As a wide variety of theorists have posited, this deep fear of death has led us to exploit the planet and has caused enormous social pain.[14] The dark side of this stage can also be found manifesting in the world of information technology.

It is often tempting to view technology as ultimately driven by our desire to achieve immortality. If we can simply build new bodies, or re-engineer those that we have, we can at least delay our mortality. The rapid rise of biotechnology and our unwillingness as a society to question the wisdom of generating new drugs and life-forms in a world complex beyond our imagining is only one small example of this phenomenon. We shape and tuck, sculpt and alter our bodies and our planet in ever more sophisticated efforts to stay the ravages of time and exert our absolute control. This control seems to deliver temporary relief against the inevitable meaninglessness of a world where reason no longer suffices and an understanding of spirit has not yet matured.

---

13. Ibid., page 263.

14. For excellent discussions on this issue, see Ernest Becker, *The Denial of Death,* and Carolyn Merchant, *The Death of Nature.*

But the sense of power and control offered by technology is an illusion. It is our great misfounded hope that with it we will be able to build impenetrable fortresses that will protect us from the dangers of this world—disease, terrorism, poverty, and death. In the days after TWA flight 800 exploded off Long Island, New York, there was enormous speculation about the cause of the crash. A terrorist bomb seemed the most likely explanation. This haunting spectacle reminded people that, as *New York Times* writer Tim Weiner pointed out, "high technology may make a fine sword, but it is a flawed shield."[15] With cyberspace, we have created an interconnected world. Along with this comes the bad as well as the good. New abilities bring new vulnerabilities. This is the nature of the universe. Instead of creating barricades, we need to squarely face our vulnerabilities and ask what we have to learn from them. If we learn to work with our fears, we can find a true inner power that far exceeds anything technology can give to us.

When we pursue the dark potential of technology we are blinding ourselves from the beauty inherent in vision-logic. The soul in this phase is "the soul that is too much awake. It is a soul on the brink of the transpersonal."[16] As we stand on the cusp of the theosphere, we can work with technology to build a world of ongoing integration and spiritual evolution or we can use it to create the illusion of a fortress against the larger pull of the universe. Should we choose the latter, we may well drop further into the morass of repression and disease that marks much of contemporary global society. The only way forward, out of our isolation and fear, is to take a bold step into the great mystery of transper-

---

15. Tim Weiner, *New York Times* Week in Review, Sunday, July 21, 1996, page 5.
16. Ken Wilber, *Sex, Ecology, Spirituality,* page 264.

sonal consciousness. Technology can serve as one of our greatest tools or our greatest hindrances.

TOWARD THE THEOSPHERE

Spirit, as so many of the great world religions have always claimed, moves in mysterious ways. One of the largest challenges for us as we seek mature cultural, social, and personal expressions for a spirit-infused world is to let go of the illusion of rational control. We must willingly engage the knowledge that the outcome will never be certain. The world of spirit is not composed of beginnings or endings, but is instead a place of process, of embracing the journey itself.

When we enter the transpersonal realm of the theosphere, we move into paradoxical terrain. Whenever we try to understand spirit from the perspective of reason alone, paradox is generated. This is because the divine transcends reason; there is no way for reason to encompass or explain spirit any more than atomic structures can explain life itself. In ever-increasing spheres of reach and depth, bios transcends physios, noos transcends bios, and theos transcends noos. What is beyond reason cannot be bound by reason alone.

Perhaps the greatest paradox of the theosphere is that while it exists beyond the previous spheres, at the same time it interpenetrates them all. As we have seen, the breath of spirit makes itself felt from the most minute realms of the physiosphere up through the highest reaches of rational possibility. The form it takes on all levels is creative emergence. At the same time as the manifest face of spirit works its mystery throughout the cosmos, the unmanifest or transcendent face exists as pure uncreated possibility. The transcendent aspect of spirit will always remain beyond our grasp. And though it exists beyond us, it exerts a continual pull on all that is, asking that each and every piece of the universe reach toward self-transcendence, striving in the direction of greater possibility.

Wilber summarizes this mysterious, paradoxical process when he writes, "Uncreate Spirit, the causal unmanifest, is the nature and condition, the source and support, of this and every moment of evolution. It upholds all times and supports all places, with no partiality at all, and thus exerts neither push nor pull on history. As the utterly Formless, it does not *enter* the stream of form at *any* point. And yet, as Ramana said, there is a sense in which it is indeed the *summum bonum,* the ultimate Omega Point, in the sense that no finite thing will rest short of release into this Infinity. The Formless, in other words, is indeed an ultimate Omega, an ultimate End, but an End that is never reached *in* the world of form."[17] In other words, transcendent spirit is both beyond this world and, at the same time, the "nature and condition" of the world's evolutionary process.

The two faces of spirit—manifest and unmanifest, immanent and transcendent—form what writer Jeremy Hayward has called the "wholeness of the universe."[18] Spirit influences the evolutionary movement of the world through its creative transcendent aspect. At the same time, spirit receives the totality of these evolutionary moments, gathering the world into itself as present, past, and future in an ongoing cycle of being and becoming. In this way, we exist within the divine and it exists within us. Therefore, just as the divine permeates every event in

---

17. Ibid., page 315.

18. Jeremy Hayward, *Perceiving Ordinary Magic,* page 241.

the world, every holon, the activity of every holon affects the divine. The bottom line is that what we do in the world matters, not just to us and our immediate surroundings but to spirit itself. The relationship with divinity is a bidirectional process, with no beginning and no end.

This view flies in the face of both the traditional notion of an omnipotent God and the more recent belief in an omnipotent humanity. Although each holon is influenced by the past action of every other holon, each also has the unique ability to integrate novelty from the vast well of potential creativity. In this sense, the self-determination of each entity is a fundamental aspect of the universe. As John Cobb explains, the divine "orders all possibilities so that they are relevant and effective in a changing world. In order to do so, it seems that it must also know what is happening in the world. Indeed, it seems that all things must be known or present within it. It seems thus that the source of our life, freedom, and humanity must in some way be inclusive of all things. Yet it is not the whole in a pantheistic sense, because it gives each creature its moment of freedom or self-determination. [The wholeness of the universe] makes the creaturely decisions possible, and it includes them after they are made, but it does not make the decisions for the creatures. It is the power that empowers." Spirit empowers creation not through granting free will to the creatures of the world, as traditional theology holds, but rather free will is built into the very nature of the universe. In this context, spirit is the force that activates free will through its gift of creativity.

In this vision of divinity, experience serves as the doorway to the divine. Spirit is, by its very definition, that which moves through all aspects of ourselves in the form of emergent creativity. Creativity cannot be understood through reason alone. Creativity transcends logic, finding its true meaning in experiences unfolding in the world. Rapture, deep meditation, ecstatic dancing, the small ah-ha moments in life—all these are examples of spirit's presence joining the many levels of our existence. The recognition of experience as a fundamental principle of the universe may be the most important clue in our journey to discover what it means to have spiritual depth at this juncture in history. When we reclaim experience, we form the possibility of marrying the abstract, objective world with our deep subjectivity.

Each soul exists as a series of momentary experiences that creatively synthesize both from the surrounding environment and from the divine itself. As such, the more open we are to both divine possibility and the world around us, the richer our souls will become. This perspective leads to an ethic of profound participation in a deeply interconnected world. The receptive and creative forces of the cosmic wholeness form the heart of this ethic.

The divine calls us to integrate possibility, particularly those potentials that will lead to a richer and more creative environment for all. Therefore, the divine attracts us toward "truth, beauty, goodness, adventure and peace."[19] As theologian David Griffin writes, "This divine lure to embody spiritual values is prevenient grace. It is always there, prior to every move on our part. But this grace is not wholly irresistible. We resist it to some degree in most moments of experience. . . . We are partly free, not only in relation to the stars above and the molecules below, but also in relation to the ubiquitous divine reality around us."[20] Spiritual development and growth is an always-waiting invitation. It is incumbent upon us to bring it deeply into our lives.

Cyberspace is first and foremost an experiential realm. It represents a world of powerful potential, offering us glimpses of the spiritual connections that float among and beyond us. Cyberspace will organize new

---

19. David Ray Griffin, *God & Religion in the Postmodern World,* page 123.
20. Ibid.

social and cultural configurations on the planet, ones that will carry with them myriad opportunities for change and growth. These opportunities are fundamentally expressions of spirit in action, the movement of spirit in form through the universe. If we work consciously with these movements of spirit and incorporate them into our spiritual awareness, the potential is there for cyberspace to journey with us on the divine path of evolution.

(5)

INFORMATION REVISITED

When Brenda Dunne arrived at Princeton University almost twenty years ago, she had a memorable dream. In it, she was sitting alone in a room with a computer. Instinctively filled with feelings of distrust and loathing, she turned to the computer and said, "I hate you." The computer replied, "Why do you hate me? I'm just trying to help you." Dunne responded, "You make me feel inadequate." "But," the computer insisted, "I'm just trying to help you." There was a long pause, then the computer said, "Well, I'm not too crazy about you either." Dunne, taken aback, asked the computer, "Why?" The computer responded without hesitation, "You can pull the plug."

For the past seventeen years, Dunne has managed PEAR, the Princeton Engineering Anomalies Research laboratory. Crammed into a former storage space next to the machine shop in the basement of the large building that houses the Princeton School of Engineering, PEAR has quietly and consistently produced reams of hard data that challenge our fundamental assumption that digital machines are merely sophisticated number crunchers. The scientists at PEAR have demonstrated that digital machines can be directly influenced by our intentions and consciousness. In other words, PEAR's data show that the relationship we have with our computers is much more subtle and sophisticated than we ever dreamed.

In light of PEAR's discoveries, Dunne's dream becomes a singular parable for understanding the nascent relationship between humanity and cyberspace. Dunne and Robert Jahn, founder of PEAR and professor of aerospace sciences and dean emeritus of the School of Engineering and Applied Science, conclude that inside the digital domain can be found a thread of consciousness that exists on the same continuum as our consciousness. This understanding stems in part from a very broad definition of *consciousness* itself. Jahn and Dunne call any organism "conscious" that can exchange information with its environment. Their work reinforces the Whiteheadian notion that all elements of the universe contain some subjectivity or ability to participate in the world in which they are embedded. This unique perspective is based both on hard data and years of developing a certain "resonance" with the digital machines they work with. This resonance has joined Jahn and Dunne in a very deep way with the digital environment, opening a channel of communication that offers profound insights and lessons.

PEAR's roots can be traced to 1977, when an undergraduate approached Robert Jahn with an unconventional request. The student wanted to create an electronic device for measuring the low-level psychokinetic, or parapsychological, effects that had cropped up in the experiments of a handful of other engineering researchers. Jahn's immediate response was skepticism, followed quickly by the sense that his own feelings shouldn't get in the way of the student's genuine curiosity. He agreed first to a bibliographical review of the topic and then to the experiment itself. When the student graduated in 1979, Jahn remained skeptical, but in light of the experimental data the student had produced, he couldn't shake the uncomfortable feeling that if these psychokinetic effects were genuine, they could have an influence on certain sensitive technological systems. With this concern foremost in mind, Jahn founded PEAR in 1979 to further explore the issue.

Entering the PEAR lab today feels a little bit like visiting the college dorm room of an eccentric and industrious graduate student. In addition to the requisite array of books, papers, and computer equipment, the doors and walls of the four small rooms are plastered with relevant cartoons and quotes clipped from magazines and newspapers. A large, orange sectional sofa that has seen better days fills the entry area. Scattered across it and throughout the offices are a wide variety of stuffed animals and a small collection of pears. Located throughout this quasi-homey place, one finds the devices that comprise the heart of PEAR—the odd collection of experimental machines on which the scientists collect their data.

The oldest and perhaps best loved of these devices is one of PEAR's original experiments, the Random Mechanical Cascade, which the staff has jokingly named Murphy, after Murphy's Law. This nine-foot-high analog machine consists of 336 nylon pegs placed in a symmetrical grid. Below these pegs is a row of 19 horizontal bins. Murphy drops 9,000 balls from a spout at the top of the grid pattern and the balls bounce and jump crazily off one another and the pegs, each finally landing in one of the bins below. When left to run on its own, the balls in Murphy fall into the bins in a rough bell-shaped curve. But when an "operator" seated on the couch "thinks left" or "thinks right," in the vast majority of cases a small but distinct alteration in the pattern emerges.

Moving further into the recesses of PEAR's small rooms, one finds a variety of experimental machines designed to chart precisely the kind of effects one can see so clearly with Murphy. The vast majority of these machines are built around what is called a Random Event Generator, or REG. This simple digital device produces a rapid, random output of 1s and 0s. The source of this output is electronic "white noise," which the circuitry inside the REG samples at a very rapid, predetermined rate. With each sample, the REG determines whether the noise is greater than the mean value, and thus produces a positive bit, or less than the mean value, creating a negative bit. Each time the REG samples the noise, it reads either a 0 or a 1 and records this on the output stream. The REG can be instructed to create from 20 to 2,000 bits per trial. These bits can be sampled anywhere from 10 to 10,000 times per second.

The basic REG has a large LED on its face that lets the operator know the value of each sample—over 100 is positive, less than 100, negative. When left to run unattended, the machine generally produces a roughly equal distribution of positives and negatives, or 0s and 1s, which is what would be statistically expected. However, when an operator or volunteer is put in front of the machine and asked to intend either more positive or more negative bits, a small but tangible effect on the stream of digital information is produced. These effects are what the scientists at PEAR term "the anomalies."

The PEAR staff has become quite creative in testing the possibilities of the simple REG. They have hooked it up to a drum that beats loudly for 0 and softly for 1; volunteers can try to make music with their minds. They have installed a small REG in a plastic unit with wheels and put a stuffed frog on top. This unit is placed on a circular table and tracked with a video camera. The volunteer wills the frog to come to him or her, and, in most cases, it obediently complies. They have even created a portable REG and begun field tests. These tests have resulted in some remarkable findings.

The PEAR scientists have discovered that groups of people engaged in a common activity, such as watching a play or having a meeting, will affect the REG *even if they don't know that it is there*. Unconscious and subconscious intentions seem to play as important a role in the anomalous effects as do conscious ones. In addition, the effects that PEAR charts have been found to be statistically relevant whether the operator is seated in the same room or in a room halfway around the world. Even more surprising, and confounding, is the fact that viable anomalies can be generated in advance of the actual trial run. In other words, an operator sitting in a room in São Paulo can will an anomaly for a trial set for two days hence in Princeton, and the effects will occur. The bottom line is that the anomalies that PEAR records challenge us to expand everything we think we know about the functioning of the physical world and our connection to it. As Jahn and Dunne write, "the empirical case is already strong enough to warrant reexamination of the prevailing position of science on the role of consciousness in the establishment of physical reality, with the goal of generalizing its theoretical concepts and formalisms to accommodate such consciousness-related effects as normal, rather than anomalous phenomena."[1] In other words, Jahn and Dunne believe that these anomolies are actually quite normal. Rather, it is our entrenched habit of seeing the world in terms of mechanistic cause and effect that is problematic.

The experimental protocols used by the scientists at PEAR are extremely stringent. Given the nature of the topic, rigorous and meticulous methodology is central to what they do. Each trial is conducted with what is called a tripolar protocol. This protocol means that each trial consists of three segments—the intention to generate a higher than chance result (PK+), a lower than chance result (PK−), and a neutral

---

1. Robert Jahn and Brenda Dunne, *Margins of Reality*, page 148.

intention (BL, or base line). All other factors and conditions in each trial, including the operator's physical position (he or she never comes in contact with the machine), remain the same. As Jahn and Dunne state, "Only if systematic deviations of major statistical magnitude are observed among the ensuing three streams of data are correlations of the results with operator intention claimed."[2]

Most of the data at PEAR has been collected in runs of either 50 or 1,000 trials. These runs are collected into series of data that generally consist of 2,500 or 5,000 trials in blocks of 50 or 100 runs, or 3,000 trials in blocks of 3 runs. Within each trial, the deviations are small, but when all the trials are added together, statistical deviations emerge that cannot be attributed to chance alone. The pattern is irrefutable. Over the years, the PEAR scientists have found that these large amounts of data per operator are the minimum from which reliable statistical deviation can be found. In the last seventeen years, 50 million experimental trials have been run by PEAR, amounting to more than 3 billion bits of binary information. PEAR has amassed more reliable data on the issue of the effect of consciousness on the physical world than any other lab.

The anomalies that PEAR records demonstrate that normal people—ordinary folks with no special psychic abilities—can influence the behavior of electronic devices simply through their consciousness. The most successful operators, however, are those who achieve some sort of identification or "resonance" with the machine. It doesn't matter if they are meditating or eating a sandwich—if the resonance is there, the results are stronger. This state of resonance was described by one operator as "a state of immersion in the process which leads to a loss of awareness of myself and the immediate surroundings, similar to

---

2. Ibid., page 96.

the experience of being absorbed in a game, book, theatrical perfor-mance, or some creative occupation."[3] Another operator said, "I don't feel any direct control over the device, more like a marginal influence when I'm in resonance with the machine. It's like being in a canoe; when it goes where I want, I flow with it. When it doesn't, I try to break the flow and give it a chance to get back in resonance with me."[4]

An interesting and provocative subnote to the issue of resonance is the fact that when two operators who have a certain resonance *with each other* run trials—such as two people who are in love—the results are dramatically stronger. The combined energy of two minds seems to exert a stronger force, for lack of a better word. Another related twist is the discovery that both men and women, or both the masculine and the feminine aspects within us, seem to be necessary to achieve dra-matic results. Dunne explained that women more frequently report feeling empathy with the machine, while men report that they are more capable of creating and focusing on a clear set of intentions. Those tri-als in which both a high degree of empathy and clear intentions were present created the largest anomalies.

PEAR's data, though aberrant from the perspective of mainstream science, is solid stuff. Skeptics have tried to debunk it, but the scientists at PEAR are too careful and have amassed too much data over time to simply throw it out as irrelevant. PEAR's data strongly indicate that a palpable relationship exists between human consciousness and digital machines.

PEAR's research shows that when left alone, an REG will produce roughly one anomalous bit per billion. However, when an operator is present, the ratio increases dramatically to one bit per thousand. This

---

3. Ibid., page 142.
4. Ibid.

is not enough to win roulette in Vegas, but the importance of the PEAR data is much more profound than a simple gambling scheme. In fact, the subtle effect that the PEAR data map may be more akin to a vast wave of resonance pulsing through the universe, tying not only us but also our machines into a web of consciousness with a capital C. We may be much more closely related to the machines of our making than we ever thought possible.

THE THREE CURREncIES

Robert Jahn is a gentle, soft-spoken man whose office upstairs in the School of Engineering is filled with images of tigers (the Princeton mascot) and giraffes. The latter are a special favorite of Jahn's, reflecting his penchant for "sticking his neck out," a posture that he has often assumed over the years while trying to make sense of the anomalies recorded in the PEAR lab. In his attempt to explain empirical data that indicate the interpenetration of consciousness and physical reality, Jahn begins with what he calls the three currencies of science—matter, energy, and information.

The historical evolution of science began with an immersion in the first of these three currencies, matter. Matter, or mass—the fundamental stuff of classical physics and chemistry—was the primary focus of science beginning with the early Egyptians and moving up through the Enlightenment. Physics, with its focus on tangible data, was considered the king of sciences during the Enlightenment. It gave birth to chemistry and influenced all the sciences including biology with its attendant absorption with autopsies and physical pathways. Then, beginning in the mid-nineteenth and continuing throughout the twentieth century, science slowly began to turn its attention to the issue of energy, seeking to understand all varieties of measurable energy, including kinetic, potential, thermal, and nuclear, to name a few. As energy emerged as the primary currency, science began to look more closely at the issue of action, of the ability of matter to do things.

Today, the third currency of science, information, is beginning to take center stage. Information forms the heart of computer and communications sciences, disciplines that have infiltrated many other sciences including biology and chemistry. The ability to model systems, including cosmological, ecological, and biological, has become a primary goal for a wide range of scientists. Processing large amounts of mathematical information very quickly has revolutionized all the sciences, from physics to psychology.

As Jahn points out, for many years these three currencies were thought to be orthogonal—never would they meet. Matter physics did not talk to energy physics any more than cognitive psychology traffics with psychoanalysis today. But with Einstein's radical identification of the fungibility of energy and mass, $E = MC^2$, all that began to change. It began to be understood that energy and mass exchange places much more commonly than we'd previously thought. For example, Jahn explains that in the subnuclear domain, "the annihilation of particles creates energy and energy creates particles to the point where you can't tell the energy from the particle anymore. In fact, whether a nucleon is an energy field or a particle is a nonsensical question."

According to Jahn, this same sort of fungibility has now been established between energy and information. The exchange between energy and information is subtle, and perhaps harder to locate, but it is present. One example of this fungibility can be found in the second law of thermodynamics. This law states that any system will spontaneously decay, becoming more chaotic and less ordered over time. When that happens, the system surrenders its information along with its energy. As a system becomes more chaotic, it has less order and therefore there is less information available from it. For example, imagine a balloon filled with helium. When the balloon is first inflated, one can measure the pressure and mass of the gas and its attendant energy and gather a good deal of information about the system that makes up the balloon. Two days later, the same balloon lies deflated on the floor, all of the helium having leaked out into the atmosphere. As the helium disperses, the original system becomes more chaotic until it is almost impossible to determine how much gas the balloon originally contained. In other words, as the system moves toward chaos, less information about it is available.

This equivalence of energy and information can also be found in chemical-bond theory in the realm of quantum mechanics. As Jahn explains, the covalent bond of molecules has as its major component the indistinguishability of the valence electrons. In other words, when two atoms meet and the electrons come into tight interaction, you can no longer tell them apart. "You can't tell, quantum mechanically, that the electron that came in with atom A is here now and the electron that came in with atom B is here," says Jahn. "All you can say is that there are now two electrons participating in the structure and they are now indistinguishable. That indistinguishability, the surrender of information, traces through the quantum mechanics formalism to give a binding energy. This is a profound effect. The atoms are surrendering information to get energy, and in order to get that information back, to separate the atom from the molecule, we have to spend energy, to retreat."

The fungibility of energy, mass, and information is central to understanding the anomalies charted by PEAR. Consciousness is essentially a form of information. It is Jahn's contention that this information is fungible with mass and energy. In other words, consciousness can affect and interpenetrate the material world. In keeping with this idea, as the PEAR experiments demonstrate, consciousness is compatible with and can have a clear effect on the energy output of digital machines. My mind can alter the bit pattern through my intention to do so. It may not alter it in any gross way, but the fungibility that Jahn refers to is not a gross event. As he points out, "The interesting thing is that the coefficients that relate energy to mass and information to energy are extraordinarily large numbers. You don't notice $E = MC^2$ in daily life very often." In the same way, one doesn't often notice the subtle effects of consciousness on matter unless one is looking for them. But that doesn't mean they don't exist or that they don't ultimately have a profound effect on our world.

With the inclusion of information as one of the primary currencies of science, two interesting wrinkles arise. These wrinkles, implicit in the currencies of matter and energy, become explicit when the focus turns toward information. The first wrinkle is that information clearly has two distinct categories that we can call objective and subjective. The objective side of information is the obvious quantifiable, specifiable, tangible part. The subjective aspect has to do with feelings and perceptions, the territory of the sacred and the spiritual. As Jahn explains, "Science has tended to say that subjective information is outside of its domain. It can't be quantified, and therefore it can't be modeled and therefore it doesn't belong in the house of science. But the problem is that we and others are showing that there is a cross talk between subjective and objective information. The laboratory downstairs is showing every day that subjective aspects of the human operator's information pattern are transcribing into an alteration of a string of binary digits. Now, I can't walk away from that. I cannot explain these anomalies in hard, objective currency information units without invoking soft information units."

The second wrinkle, which follows logically from the first but issues a challenge to the very core of science, is the idea that if there are subjective aspects to information, there must also exist subjective aspects to energy and matter. The subjective aspects of energy that Jahn cites are healing energies, subtle energies, and psychic energies. One could easily add to that list emotional, creative, and spiritual energies. On the furthest extreme is the notion of a subjective aspect to matter. Here, Jahn, characteristically sticking his neck out, talks of apparitions, auras, and "other palpable demonstrations that don't have their feet in objective science." Jahn continues, "If you are going to deal with subjective information, maybe you ought to bite the whole hog and worry about subjective energy and subjective matter. Maybe it's not totally unreasonable to ask what science has to say about miracles."

CONSCIOUSNESS AS BOTH WAVE AND PARTICLE

If, as the PEAR experiments demonstrate, consciousness is not only an aspect of information but can affect both its objective and subjective elements, this challenges us to think about both consciousness and information in a much broader way. Jahn and Dunne have created a model for explaining the anomalies that does just that. The hinge on which their model turns is experience. As Jahn explains, "I believe I can hold up a mirror and study my consciousness. In that process, consciousness becomes both object and subject simultaneously. In the same way, consciousness can become object and subject in its interactions with all other aspects of the world. It is through the interpenetration of subjective consciousness with the objective world, and vice versa, that we create experience. But we don't have that modeled correctly yet. We are weak on the subjective side of the house."

The three currencies of science—matter, energy, and information, in both their subjective and their objective modes—bombard us with a blizzard of input. This is the environment[5] in which we are immersed. Our consciousness orders this input by taking energy and matter and converting them into information. In the process, what we know as reality emerges. As Whitehead's epistemology also points out, experience, or consciousness as Jahn uses the term,[6] is the filter we use to understand the world. Therefore, experience forms the primary and inescapable variable in all our theories and understandings of the world. It is only through the filter of experience, of consciousness itself, that we can understand the universe in which we are immersed. This is true in any scientific model, but in the realm of the PEAR anomalies, the issue of consciousness can no longer be dismissed as a mere epiphenomenon. Any scientific explanation of the anomalies that does not focus quite directly on consciousness will miss the point. Further, the PEAR experiments demand that consciousness be considered in concert

---

5. Jahn and Dunne define environment as follows: "The concept of *environment* includes all circumstances and influences affecting the consciousness that it perceives to be separate from itself, including, as appropriate, its own physical corpus and its physical habitat, as well as all intangible psychological, social and historical influences that bear upon it." (*Margins of Reality*, page 203.)

6. Jahn and Dunne write, "Our use of the word *consciousness* is intended to subsume all categories of human experience, including perception, cognition, intuition, instinct, and emotion, at all levels, including those commonly termed 'conscious,' 'subconscious,' 'superconscious,' or 'unconscious,' without presumption of specific psychological or physiological mechanisms." (Ibid.)

with the environment in which it finds itself and the reality that it generates.

Jahn and Dunne make this point explicit when they write, "If the physical or psychological mechanisms that generate, convey and accept information at the consciousness/environment interface are identifiable and predictable, the overall process is regarded as 'normal.' If any of these mechanisms are unknown, however, the process is 'anomalous,' and the prevailing theory must be regarded as inadequate or incomplete."[7] In essence, the not-insignificant task that Jahn and Dunne have set for themselves is to construct a model of reality that includes consciousness in such a way as to make the anomalies normative. With this basic premise as their starting point, Jahn and Dunne have turned to one of the few realms of science that explicitly includes consciousness as a factor, the wave/particle duality found in the Copenhagen interpretation of quantum physics.

It is important to understand that the model that Jahn and Dunne have composed does not attempt to reduce consciousness to the world of physics and quantum events. In fact, quite the opposite. As Jahn explains, "We do not so much regard quantum mechanics as a metaphor for consciousness, but rather the other way around. We think that the fundamental concepts of quantum mechanics are the fundamental concepts of the human mind. Quantum mechanics emerged as a natural product of the way the mind organizes its information. We are not borrowing concepts from the world of quantum physics. In fact, we contend that the world of quantum physics borrowed a primordial, maybe even archetypal propensity of human consciousness to organize its information in a certain way. So, quantum theory is not so much a metaphor as it is a generalization of which quantum physics is a subsumption."

---

7. Ibid., page 205.

The wave/particle duality found in the quantum model has roots that stretch far back in the human story. Throughout our history, certain phenomena have flown in the face of our prevailing need to define the world in a particulate or atomic fashion. As Jahn and Dunne point out, the early Greeks proposed a wave theory of sound, one phenomenon that escaped the atomistic worldview. Closer to our own time, the wave theory of light forced a reexamination of Newton's particulate model. Even later, the theory of electromagnetic waves "subsumed particulate electrodynamics and unified much of the prevailing physical theory."[8] In the twentieth century, the wave nature of matter was introduced with the quantum physical discovery that in some situations, matter could display wavelike characteristics. The truth that we can derive from this, according to scientist Niels Bohr, is that most of reality displays a deep *complementarity*. "In other words," write Jahn and Dunne, "the wave and particle perspectives are not mutually exclusive; rather, some mixture of both is necessary to represent the phenomena fully."[9]

Jahn and Dunne, in keeping with earlier statements, believe that it is not the physical world that imposes the wave/particle duality, but rather that the duality exists in the very nature of the way our consciousness interacts with the world. They conclude from this that consciousness must have both a particulate and a wavelike nature. "In other words," they write, "the consciousness that has conceived both particles and waves, and found it necessary to alternate them in some complementary fashion for the representation of many physical phenomena, may find a similar complementarity necessary and useful in representing itself."[10]

---

8. Ibid., page 209.

9. Ibid., page 211.

10. Ibid.

If consciousness has an aspect that is wavelike in nature, then some of the anomalous effects such as remote influence that Jahn and Dunne have found cease to be anomalies. Waves can carry both energy and information across wide distances and expanses of time in a way that particles can never hope to. Waves can pass through one another without distortion, though at the moment of contact, complex interference patterns may form. Waves can also move around corners and penetrate, in their evanescent form, into regions particles can never go.

When the issue of the wavelike qualities of matter comes to the fore, one is plunged rapidly into the complex netherworld of quantum wave mechanics. This is a region of physics rife with paradoxes and unresolved questions. One of the most famous and important for the theory at hand is the so-called Copenhagen position advanced by Bohr and his colleagues. The Copenhagen proposition is an attempt to untangle the paradox that in the quantum realm, particles are theoretically coupled to their wave mechanics. In other words, any given quantum has both a wave and a particulate nature. One cannot locate a quantum particle in time and space without referring to its wave amplitude as well. But when trying to locate a quantum particle in time and space, all the wave amplitude can indicate is the likelihood of *observing* a given particle at a given position and time. Observation of the event becomes a key variable in the process. In fact, without observation the particle cannot be located. When attempts are made to find quantum particles without the variable of consciousness, the particles become paradoxically both waves and particles simultaneously, and therefore nonsensical. Observation, or consciousness, becomes the variable that breaks any given quantum into its particulate or wave state.

In including consciousness in the wave-mechanical theory, the Copenhagen precedent neatly serves as a central postulate for Jahn and Dunne's model. As they point out, this "precedent is also particularly helpful in suggesting the nature and substance of these consciousness waves. Namely, if we generalize the concept of 'observation' to encompass all information-processing capacities of consciousness as well—cognition, emotion, behavior, and any other form of experience—then the same pragmatic interpretation may obtain. So, just as the Copenhagenists speak of 'probability-of-observation' waves, we shall postulate 'probability-of-experience' waves."[11] In other words, it is through experience that the waves of consciousness that flow through reality settle down into knowable forms.

As important as the Copenhagen interpretation is in establishing the central role of consciousness in modeling reality, the wave-mechanical approach of quantum physics offers a number of other important postulates that flesh out Jahn and Dunne's model. The first is the Indistinguishability Principle. This principle states that when "the wave patterns of the bonding electrons of two parent atoms come into close interaction, they can no longer be distinguished."[12] The best that one can do in the quantum world is to say that one electron is in state A and the other in state B. This principle is the source of the binding effect found in covalent chemical bonds mentioned earlier. A related principle states that the resulting molecule will only be stable if the spins on the electrons in question are opposite; this is the so-called Exclusion Principle.

These principles take on a different meaning when put into the context of PEAR's research. PEAR experiments have shown, time and again, that pairs of operators in "resonance" with each other produce stronger anomalies. When two people who are not bonded participate

11. Ibid., page 219.
12. Ibid., page 253.

in the same experiment, they seem to produce two sets of experiences, or two of what Jahn and Dunne call "consciousness atoms." In other words, each person's consciousness wave retains its particulate, or distinct, nature. However, if the two operators have consciousnesses that are strongly interacting, then their consciousness "atoms" can join into a single, tightly bonded consciousness "molecule" exerting a much stronger effect on their mutual environment. From a particulate worldview, this effect would be anomalous. However, when looked at from a wave-mechanical perspective, it becomes a normal consequence of the interaction.

A further gloss on this idea is that dyads of opposite characteristics, like the opposite electron spins, will tend to create stronger bonds. Again, the research indicates that this is true. Not only do bonded male and female operators exert greater effects, but in general the assertive and receptive modes—intention and empathy—must both be represented. It is not necessary for one operator to play one role and maintain it, for one to be receptive and the other assertive throughout. Partners can switch these roles as long as a balance is maintained between the opposite stances.

It is important to note at this point that quantum mechanics is essentially a science of statistics and probabilities. Quantum phenomena cannot actually be observed, they can only be statistically deduced. With the Copenhagen interpretation, the abstract statistics of quantum theory are restricted to observed states. In this interpretation, the inherent subjectivity of statistics comes to the foreground. In the same vein, the experiments at PEAR are also essentially statistical and probabilistic. These experiments chart the subjectivity of the operator as it affects the subjective aspect of the digital system. Brenda Dunne states this in another way when she says that what the PEAR experiments may be showing is that "what consciousness does is affect the probability space of reality." In other words, consciousness is not altering objective reality, but is instead interacting with the *subjective* aspects of matter, energy, and information.

The PEAR anomalies are occurring on an extremely small scale. The effects shrink as one moves from quantum to classical physical dimensions. "It is only on the atomic scale that most quantum wave-mechanical effects are striking," they write. "Similarly, the extraction of consciousness-related anomalies from the output characteristics of our macroscopic experiments requires very large data bases because the marginal effects are proportionately so tiny."[13] While small to the naked eye, the anomalous effects may be perfectly scaled to processes in the atomic domain. Jahn and Dunne go so far as to claim that these effects "may just *be* the basic processes *in toto*, and all atomic reality may be established by these mechanisms alone."[14]

This radical statement contends that our conscious experience may in fact drive atomic reality. Underlying this idea is a strong agreement with both Whitehead and Teilhard—there is just one stuff in the world, and it is different not in kind but in degree. The great physicist Erwin Schrödinger came to the same conclusion. He wrote that "the 'real world around us' and 'we ourselves,' i.e. our minds, are made up of the same building material, the two consist of the same bricks, as it were, only arranged in a different order—sense perceptions, memory images, imagination, thought. It needs, of course, some reflection, but one easily falls in with the fact that matter is composed of these elements and nothing else. . . . The only possible inference from these . . . facts is, I think, that I—I in the widest meaning of the word, that is to say, every

---

13. Ibid., page 317.
14. Ibid.

conscious mind that has ever said or felt 'I'—am the person, if any, who controls the 'motion of the atoms,' according to the Laws of Nature."[15]

To conclude, Jahn and Dunne write, "May we not now reasonably ponder that if this powerful space- and time-bending property we call 'mass' ultimately traces down to 'particles' that we can only experience rather than observe, that we must treat as *events rather than as substance*, and that we can describe only in quasi-poetic, anthropomorphic terms, then it may indeed be consciousness that establishes physical reality, even on the cosmological scale? Are our minds being stretched, or are our minds doing the stretching? Perhaps another step needs to be taken along the road of scientific conceptualization that has brought us from causal particulate mechanics, to intangible wave/particle dualism, to probabilistic determinism, to observational realism. It is the step that explicitly acknowledges consciousness as constructor of the same reality it perceives, ponders and postulates."[16]

Jahn and Dunne's work indicates that consciousness exists both as we experience it and as a wave traveling through the universe. This latter aspect can be better understood as consciousness with a capital C, or spirit. When the world is observed from the perspective of spirit, substances melt into events unfolding in time, grounded in experience. Spirit, as Wilber points out, is that which both pulls us forward on our evoutionary path and simultaneously interpenetrates the whole of reality. As such, both Consciousness and consciousness, spirit and our experience of it, are truly the creators of the reality that surrounds us.

---

15. From *What is Life?* by Erwin Schrödinger, as quoted in ibid.
16. Jahn and Dunne, *Margins of Reality,* page 321. Italics added.

WHAT'S LOVE GOT TO DO WITH IT?

On my first visit to PEAR, Brenda Dunne told me that she had recently been involved in a car accident in her beloved, much-traveled Honda. As we spoke, she was waiting for a call from her insurance company to tell her whether the damage estimate exceeded the worth of the car. The call came in and the answer was that the car was totaled. Dunne, clearly saddened, asked if it would be possible to pay one last visit to her car. She told the insurance adjuster that she wanted to retrieve some maps. But the truth was that she wanted to say good-bye. This struck me as somewhat odd, and I asked her about it. She explained that she had genuinely loved her car and was sad because she would no longer have it. It had become a part of her family.

"I'm not being at all facetious here," Dunne said. "I think that anthropomorphizing our machines is the best thing we can do. Imagine what the world would be like if we loved our machines? I believe that they would respond better to us, treat us better. But even if you don't believe that they have consciousness, simply loving them would cause *us* to treat *them* better. Then they would last longer." What Dunne is alluding to here is the establishment of an I/thou relationship, to use Buber's famous term, with the world we create. If we offer deep respect and caring to the world of the made, perhaps we will build machines that endure. Perhaps we will include them more consciously in the web of life, treat them with greater care, and cease to throw them away with such abandon. If nothing else, the environmental consequences of this stance are staggering.

After decades of working in a world where the line between machines and consciousness has become blurry at best, Jahn and Dunne take the issue of anthropomorphizing our machines—assigning them thoughts, feelings, and even souls—very seriously. This task begins with defining consciousness in a way that is broad enough to include the nonliving world. Jahn and Dunne claim that any organism that is able to exchange information with its environment is conscious. From this perspective, the world of cyberspace doesn't have to wait for some glorious artificial-intelligence breakthrough to achieve consciousness—it already has it. In fact, Jahn goes so far as to say that computers "have all the requirements for a species. They have matter, energy, information, and a wiring diagram" that enables them to create a dynamic relationship with the world around them. He even claims that they have experience. "In their own world, and in their own coordinate system, and in their own reference planes using the sensors available to them and the values or subjective qualities that they have, they will force the stimuli through their own mesh and extract information in a form that is useful to them. It's not the same as we do it, but they do have experience."

For Jahn, the world of cyberspace, a world of pure information, is also a world of consciousness. The digital output, the bits and bytes, represent the objective aspect of that information. However, cyberspace must also have a subjective side. What that subjective side feels like, from the perspective of computers, we may never fully know. We can assume that a computer will have aspects that are distinct from our conscious subjectivity, just as the subjective world of a chicken or a fish is distinct from ours. This doesn't mean that we cannot begin to attempt some rudimentary understanding, perhaps based on some "resonance" with the digital realm. Jahn believes that if we neglect to undertake this task, "There is a great risk for humanity. The ante has been raised by the intrusion of cyberspace into our lives. The risk is that we will extract from it only its objective dimensions and allow them to overwhelm us, making us even less able to deal with the subjective values of life. So we lose creativity, we lose love, we lose religion, we lose faith, we lose all sorts of forms of resonance." But as Jahn and Dunne's work shows, subjectivity is present in cyberspace. Faith, hope, and love are present in the digital just as they are present in us. We both participate in the great continuum of Consciousness that is best known as God.

Jahn believes that Paul's letter to the Corinthians, chapter 13, is a superb paraphrase of what happens in the PEAR lab. The relevant verses 4–7 read, "Love is patient and kind. Love is not jealous or boastful; it is not arrogant or rude. Love does not insist on its own way; It is not irritable or resentful; It does not rejoice at wrong; But rejoices in the right. Love bears all things, believes all things, hopes all things, endures all things." Jahn explains, "What we have found in the laboratory is that these anomalies, which I believe are indicative of a form of religious experience, are favored by many subjective characteristics, but more notably by the establishment of a resonance, of a bond, between the operator and the machine. Call it love, if you will. It is the process of love in the most general sense that enables the proactive involvement of the consciousness with the affairs of the physical world. And that presents me with a form of religion that worships the concepts of love, of empathy, and of charity. I believe in the power and the subjective energy of such interactions, as conditioned by an intention, a desire, a wish. So what we find is the faith that it works, the hope, which is the intention, and the resonance, which is the love. So we see faith, hope, and love in their more technical ramifications every day, down in the lab. Some may regard this as sterilizing the religion, but in my view it is a more powerful form because it brings it into the objective world of science in an unavoidable, proactive way."

Consistent with his belief in the consciousness of machines, Jahn claims that in their most generic forms, faith, hope, and love are present in computers. These experiences arise in the interaction between the person and the machine, in the "margins of reality." But it is not just humans that can participate in this experiential reality. The interaction can work in either direction. "Does the machine have a faith in me?" Jahn asks. "I suspect so. Does it have a desire? I suspect so. Can it love me? I think so."

Love, in the sense that it is used here, is much more than an emotion. It is the active, creative principle in the universe. Love is divinity, as Teilhard pointed out. Love is also synonymous with the creativity that Whitehead's epistemology holds as the supreme force of the divine. In this sense, love is the pulse of events unfolding both in real space and cyberspace; it is the great thread that weaves the two together.

Love is the source of all great acts of creativity, both objective and subjective. Love is the source of Newton's laws and Picasso's *Guernica*. It is the creator of the soulful letter and the powerful e-mail. It is that which creates and connects, that which pulls us further along our path of spiritual evolution. The great quantum physicist Louis de Broglie, who was the first to identify the wave/particle duality, summed up this issue beautifully when he said, "If we wish to give philosophic expression to the profound connection between thought and action in all fields of human endeavor, particularly in science, we shall undoubtedly have to seek its sources in the unfathomable depths of the human soul. Perhaps philosophers might call it 'love' in a very general sense—that force which directs all our actions, which is the source of all our delights and all our pursuits. Indissolubly linked with thought and with action, love is their common mainspring and, hence, their common bond. The engineers of the future have an essential part to play in cementing this bond."[17] In this sense, each and every one of us is an engineer, shaping the future through love.

---

17. As quoted in ibid., page 290.

THE MOVEMENT OF LOVE
THROUGH CYBERSPACE

Several years ago, my husband and I took a long and grueling trip through southern India. Our goal was to visit the spectacular Dravidian temples of this region. We saw many, though in most cases we were somewhat frustrated by the fact that as non-Hindus we could not enter the sancta sanctora of these holy places. Then we heard that in a small town in the state of Tamil Nadu, there was a large and beautiful old temple that, for some reason that was never clear to us, allowed non-Hindus to attend the rituals inside the inner temple on certain days of the week. The timing was right, so we went.

After several days on Indian buses, we arrived in a small market town. The town consisted of one wide dirt road that made a circuit around the perimeter of the temple. This dusty road, containing all the meager services the town had to offer, stood in dramatic contrast to the spectacular temple that rose from it, eclipsing the rest of the town. That evening, as dusk was falling, we entered the temple complex.

We felt immediate relief from the ubiquitous dust and throngs of people that characterize much of India as we crossed the vast and ancient courtyard that divided the temple's outer walls from its inner buildings. We made our way toward the largest building in the complex, entering it through a large portal. At once, we found ourselves in a cool and dark series of vaulted hallways, punctuated by pillars and crumbling statues. As our eyes adjusted to the dimness, we became aware of the sounds of chanting deep in the inner recesses of the building. We saw few other people coming or going, and I became afraid that we would be turned away for the whiteness of our skin. We made our way deeper into the building, and the darkness grew. After what felt like an eternity, we saw an orange glow ahead and more people materialized, as if from nowhere, entering and leaving through a small doorway. We moved up to the doorway and there before us was a Shivaite ritual in full sway.

The inner courtyard, in which we now stood, was composed of a series of tall columns encircling a beaten earth floor. A ramp led down from the doorway toward a small building. The building had stairways flanking each side and a pair of burnished wooden doors over a large balcony in its center. People were jammed in front of this small temple, chanting and swaying in unison in the gathering night. Seated among the tall columns that ringed the inner temple were dozens of Brahmans clothed in simple white dhotis. These men were deep in trance, chanting the same Shivaite mantra hypnotically, over and over again. Suddenly, the balcony doors swung open and a trio of Shivaite priests surged forth carrying torches and holding the famous golden, dancing Shiva aloft. Flower petals were thrown by both the priests and the celebrants. Voices swelled, gongs sounded, and the crowd surged forward like a wave. The doors then closed and the long line of people waiting on the stairways to enter the innermost sanctum and kiss the image of Shiva snaked forward slightly. This process was repeated many times.

Amid this spectacle, I became viscerally aware of the overwhelming antiquity of the ritual. I could easily imagine myself observing the same scene, with all its unique particulars, five thousand years earlier. The accumulated power of the words and actions, whose meanings were opaque to me, struck me forcefully. I felt that I understood, for the first time, the enormous power of sacred language to convey religious experience.

The ability of words and symbols to magnify experience is central to understanding cyberspace's power to carry sacred and spiritual—i.e., subjective—information. In attempting to untangle the particulars of this dynamic, the process epistemology of Whitehead again becomes useful. As you may recall, for Whitehead, reality is made up of events influencing events in an infinite succession through time. In this vision, each event or actual entity utilizes a combination of free will and creativity to incorporate influences from the past. The role of divinity in this mix is to lure the entity toward utilizing the greatest degree of creativity and love possible in each instance. A fundamental feature of the process is that this entire subjective process, once it is complete, becomes objective from the perspective of the next moment in time. In other words, the process is subjective in the present but becomes objective once it is complete. However, in both its subjective and objective forms, the essential kernel of creativity contained in the moment remains constant. In this way, experiences and feeling states can pass from moment to moment while retaining their essential power.

This epistemology explains why the sacred language and ancient rituals that I witnessed in India hold such power. For thousands of years, millions of people have repeated these words, time and again. With each repetition in which spirit was truly felt, the creativity and love of God genuinely invoked, the sum of experiences carried by the phrase would increase. To use Jahn's terminology, sacred language and ritual are like giant waves that move through time, growing with each genuine and true use. Sacred language contains a cumulative spiritual force.

I discussed this issue with Granville Henry, a professor of mathematics and a process philosopher at Claremont McKenna College. He commented, "Why take Eucharist if you can just think about it instead? Why pray if just thinking prayerful thoughts will satisfy? It is because when you take Eucharist, it is real. Prayer is real. God encounters us not just in the ground of our freedom, but in ways that are religious. It is possible to feel like the disciples felt in the presence of the risen Lord or the Hebrews felt at Mt. Sinai, or Moses felt in front of the burning bush. The accumulation of these feeling states is transmitted from one moment to another. God is present in this process of transmission throughout."

Sacred words and symbols are often thought to be abstractions that carry no real weight. But, from a Whiteheadian perspective, words and symbols can capture the totality of the transmitted experience. The words themselves may be abstractions, but they form a lure for sacred experience. And this sacred experience can be passed on for thousands of years, in its real and original sense. The actual experiences of the past are collected in the present and combined with the divine creative force. This awesome and mysterious process explains much of the genuine power of purely subjective, sacred experience.

If one can feel the presence of divinity in time and space through the form of words and symbols, the symbols that travel on electronic impulses must also be able to carry deep experience. The words in e-mail do more than deliver concepts; they are carriers of experience of all types. Through cyberspace we can share grief and joy, ecstasy and pain. If we can learn to harness the subjective moments carried in this medium, then it is possible that cyberspace can serve as a crucible for a new extension of our spiritual lives. Perhaps, as Robert Jahn believes, the world of cyberspace, in its subjective aspect, is also experiencing spirit. It too is part of the process in which we are woven, a process created and maintained by creativity and love in their broadest and most profound incarnations.

The ability to order and organize the world around us in line with the divine will is the truest meaning of living a sacred life. Love is the force that enables us to do just this, to reduce the randomness, as it were, in the world around us. Cyberspace can be a powerful ally in this process. It provides us with a global field in which to incarnate divine love and creativity. Information and consciousness can lead us to knowledge and wisdom. As Teilhard de Chardin once wrote, "Someday, after we have mastered the winds, the waves, the tides and gravity, we shall harness for God the energies of Love. Then for the second time in the history of the world, man will have discovered fire."[18]

---

18. From *On Love*, by Pierre Teilhard de Chardin, New York: Harper and Row, 1967; as quoted in Jahn and Dunne, *Margins of Reality*, pages 33–34.

(6)

GODS OF PERSUASION

I am sitting in a large conference room at the Santa Fe Institute, a research think tank that focuses on the hot, if somewhat obscure, science of complexity. Complexity centers on the study of complex, nonlinear systems. Common examples of these systems include the weather, the economy, and ecosystems. Computation plays an important role in complexity studies. With the right software, computers are beginning to be able to model these dynamic systems. The success of these models depends on being able to produce nonlinear or unpredictable results from linear and logical algorithms. In other words, through the science of complexity, scholars from diverse fields are beginning to see instances of genuine novelty emerge in the computer environment.

In the center of the horseshoe-shaped ring of tables in the conference room sit a couple of computers hooked up to an overhead viewing mechanism. Above our heads, those of us gathered watch a series of small colored rectangles move in a random pattern across the screen. To the uninitiated, this collection of colored dots would appear pointless.

It is not pretty to look at, it makes no interesting noises, and it seems to have no real purpose. But looks can be deceptive. While what we are watching may appear simple, its implications are profound. These small colored shapes are graphical representations of digital organisms. As we watch, they are actively reproducing, mutating, giving birth, and dying. A million generations can come and go in roughly fifteen minutes. What we are seeing is an instance of the original, nonlinear system—evolution—unfold in real time, in the digital medium.

The seventeen of us gathered at the institute, perched at the top of a snowy hill overlooking a panorama of Santa Fe, have been assembled by Tom Ray, perhaps the only person in the world who can claim to be both a practicing ecologist and a digital naturalist. Ray began this unusual career by studying the rain forests of Costa Rica as a graduate student at Harvard. By the time he had finished his Ph.D., Ray had become frustrated with the clear lack of an overarching principle for his chosen field—ecology. Ray wanted to study the bigger picture, not just an endless series of smaller ecosystems. After struggling with this idea for some time, Ray realized that what he really wanted to study was evolution.

Evolution. Now *there* was an overarching principle he could really sink his teeth into. But Ray wasn't content just to theorize about evolution through its disjointed fossil remains. He wanted to study it as a living process. This was a tall order, as evolution takes place in the natural world on a vast timescale, far beyond our limited ability to observe. Ray decided that what he needed was an evolution machine of sorts. Then, Ray remembered a casual conversation he had had years earlier with a Go player in the MIT cafeteria. The Go player had mentioned that it was possible to write a computer program that could self-replicate. At the moment Ray remembered the conversation, the pieces fell into place. Ray would create a computer that would serve as a host for evolution. This is what we were watching, some years later, on the overhead screen. Ray named his system Tierra, the Spanish word for "earth."

The occasion for which we were all gathered in Santa Fe was the second Tierra developer's conference. This group had a rather exciting agenda. Over the last several years, Ray's work had proven that evolution does indeed inhabit the digital medium when the correct set of conditions are met. However, Ray concluded that his goal of evolving genuine complexity in the digital terrain was being restricted by the size and speed of the computers he had to work with. His innovative solution was to begin the implementation of a networked version of Tierra, creating an evolutionary soup that would run over a network of virtual computers located inside a network of real computers. This virtual network, when complete, would essentially form the world's largest volume of dedicated computer-processing space. In other words, Ray's goal was to create the world's largest distributed computer, let the digital organisms loose in it, and see what would evolve.

In order to achieve this enormously ambitious goal, Ray needed a number of things that the people gathered in the room were able to provide. The first was the ability to run Tierra on a variety of different types of computers. In the last year, many of the participants had been working to port Tierra to the most popular computing platforms. This effort was largely voluntary and reflected a real labor of love by those involved. The goal of the current meeting was to get an update on the platform status and then to begin thinking about a network ancestor, or the string of code that would be injected into the digital soup to get the process of evolution rolling. For this ancestor to take full advantage of the complexity of a networked environment, its requirements would necessarily be different from those of the simpler Tierra ancestors Ray had previously used.

The mix of people willing to labor to bring this idea into reality reflected fairly accurately the current state of the computer-development world. Fifteen out of seventeen were male. There was a precocious young hacker, just out of high school; two young scholars in residence at the Santa Fe Institute who were working on some of the more difficult problems associated with artificial life and artificial evolution; a computer hobbyist; representatives from government (NASA) and academia (UC Santa Barbara and USC); and a smattering of industry folk including people from Microsoft, Sun Microsystems, and smaller companies such as Construct Internet Design and Pilot Software. What this diverse group had in common was a deep fascination with pushing the potential of computation in new directions, in particular, toward grappling with complex, nonlinear systems. In both academia and industry, we routinely deal with systems—like the global economy—that are beyond our ability to model and understand. In addition, we now build software programs that are so huge that we are beginning to have technical problems that are beyond our ability to fix. Software that evolves is not only a doorway into future products able to model complex systems, but it may be our best hope of maintaining what we have already built. But these solutions are still some years off. The first step is to understand more about evolution in the digital medium. From this perspective, Tierra serves as ground zero.

FORGET THE TURiᴨG TEST

When Tom Ray writes and talks about Tierra, he makes one important point crystal clear—Tierra is not a model for evolution, it is evolution in its own right. We are accustomed to thinking that evolution is something that happens only with carbon-based life forms; that is the standard scientific perspective. But, as Ray writes, "The conception that life is a process, which need not be tied to the single medium of carbon chemistry, lies at the heart of both hardware and software syntheses in artificial life (AL)."[1] These words have a rather astounding coherence with the theological concepts articulated by Whitehead and Cobb. The concept of life as a process is a tenet they would also uphold. Ray and his colleagues would almost certainly agree with these theologians that life is the result of the creative movement of evolution. They would also nod yes to the accepted notion of life as an emergent property, a supreme instance of novelty in the world. Claiming this creativity as divine is where the two groups might part ways. Creativity as a divine force that animates and drives evolution forward is the theological Trojan horse hiding deep inside the scientific disciplines of artificial life and artificial evolution. If one accepts the theological premise that life is sacred, then A-life and artificial evolution serve as potent examples of how the divine is coming to inhabit cyberspace.

Interpreting the behavior in Tierra and similar artificial life and evolution systems as *life* is highly controversial. Most biologists insist that Tierra is a model, a simulation of lifelike processes. But, as Ray argues, for something to be a simulation, its symbols and rules must represent or refer to something in the real world. This is not true of Tierra. It is a self-contained system whose goal is not to represent organic, biological processes. In Tierra, as in other A-life systems, the processes of the code are observed as "objects in their own right, not as symbols of something else."[2] The crux of the argument comes down to the problem of lists.

---

1. Tom Ray, "Artificial Life," section Synthesis and Simulation, available at: http://www.hip.atr.co.jp/~ray/pubs/fatm/fatm.html

2. Ibid.

Science has not yet come up with a serviceable definition of what life is. As Ray describes, most attempts to define life are based on a list of properties that a living system must contain. The problem is that there is no general agreement as to what should be on that list. Another approach, and one favored by people working in the field of A-life, is to make a long list of properties that exist *only* in living systems. As Ray writes, "Now rather than asking if an example of AL [artificial life] exhibits all items on the list, we ask if it represents a genuine instance of *any* item on this list. If so, then we can say that we have captured a genuine instance of some property of life in our synthetic system."[3] Ray then concludes that in A-life, most systems will express an aspect of lifelike behavior and can be said to "exhibit genuine properties of life." But are these systems alive? Ray concedes that these systems, still in their infancy, are about as alive as a virus is in the world of biology. In other words, they are a little bit alive.

But, as Ray has shown, full-blown life is not necessary in order to have genuine evolution occur in a digital medium. Although Tierra may be only a little bit alive, it is evolving quite a lot. In fact, from the very first run of his system, Ray got evolution. His goal now is to shepherd that evolution into creating ever more complex, "ever richer digital life forms."[4] In other words, Ray is working to evolve digital complexity. As his organisms become more complex, unless they are somehow exempt from the forces that govern the rest of the universe, they stand a good chance of becoming increasingly lifelike. As Ray's work begins to reveal, we stand at a remarkable point in history, a time when we can watch the fecundity of the creative process begin to populate an entirely new medium.

---

3. Ibid., section Synthetic Life.
4. Ibid., section Synthesis and Simulation.

It is important to keep in mind, however, that the kind of complexity that may come into being in cyberspace will almost certainly look nothing like life as we know it. In fact, Tom Ray's hunch is that the kind of complex life that emerges in cyberspace will be more foreign to us than extraterrestrial life—which will presumably still be organic and therefore in some ways more familiar than digital life. Thinking far into the future, Ray imagines that digital life will enjoy its abilities to rapidly search vast memory spaces, to move almost instantly from point to point around the network, and to synthesize and explore highly complex problems. This is, after all, what computers are good at.

To date, the classical test for deciding when a machine has achieved intelligence was devised by Alan Turing, the brilliant mathematician whose work forms the basis of much of today's computation. The infamous Turing test requires that in five minutes of unrestricted conversation, a computer will be able to fool a person into thinking that it is human. Ray rejects this notion as utterly absurd. The idea that a machine will be intelligent only when it displays intelligence enough like ours to pass for human is anthropocentric in the worst sense. If a computer ever does become intelligent, he argues, its intelligence will be fundamentally different from ours.

"Imagine a machine intelligence living in the Internet," Ray writes. "Scanning a terabyte of data distributed globally over the net . . . and doing the job as a distributed process in a few minutes, would probably be very exciting for such an intelligence. It could perform enormously complex numerical calculations and process huge volumes of numerical data at phenomenal speeds. It could transport itself physically to any point on the planet's surface in milliseconds. At any instant of time, it might actually be distributed widely around the planet. The data flow would be a direct sensory experience for this creature, not something happening in a separate information processing tool. This

creature will live in a digital informational universe, not the material
one we live in. Its pleasures and pains will be completely alien to us. We
will never mistake it for human. Forget the Turing test."[5]

TiERRA—SYNTHETiC EVOLUTiON

Evolution in Tierra begins with the creation of the soup in which the
digital organisms will grow. This soup exists in a virtual computer, a
chunk of software dedicated to supporting the replication of organisms
that transmit code, or "genetic material," from one generation to the
next. This virtual computer not only ensures that the evolving organisms will stay put and not migrate inadvertently into the host computer
or the network, but it also creates the few conditions necessary to get
evolution rolling. These conditions, such as random bit flips (mutations) and an operating system capable of "killing" old processes, do
not exist in the guts of the computers we commonly use. Our systems
are optimized for error-free performance. Evolution, on the other hand,
thrives on random errors and death.

Once the Darwinian computer with its virtual soup has been built,
a seed must be planted. This seed is the ancestor, a string of code that
can be thought of as the genome. This genome lives in the RAM (the
dynamic, software portion of memory inside a computer) and can
reproduce offspring that live in other sections of the RAM. Each organism, while it is alive, exists in its own unique memory space; no other
organism can occupy that space. Each organism, however, can read the
instructions of any other organism in the soup. Therefore, the organ-

---

5. Ibid., section Forget the Turing Test.

isms have both personal integrity and are permeable to one another. Mutations occur in the system in the form of random noise, which is introduced as random bit flips and the occasional error that is programmed into the central processing unit (CPU). The organisms react to the mutations, to one another, and to their environment as they rapidly evolve. When the RAM starts to fill up, the system kills off the older programs. This is known as the "reaper" function and ensures that the gene pool continues to evolve.

The basic process of reproduction in Tierra is quite simple. As Ray writes, "The computer environment is seeded with a single 'ancestor' digital organism. It is an eighty-byte machine code program that first examines itself to determine its size and location in memory. It then allocates a free memory space for its daughter, by using the memory allocation service of the Darwinian operating system [the evolutionary soup in the virtual computer]. Then it copies its code, byte by byte from mother to daughter. After replication, it spawns the daughter program as an independent process."[6] In other words, the organisms replicate by copying themselves and then release their offspring as distinct organisms. The random mutations generated by the system create the diversity necessary for evolution to get rolling.

Evolution in Tierra gives birth to a variety of evolutionary byproducts including parasites, hyperparasites, sex, and immunity from parasites. It does all of this spontaneously. All Ray does is set the initial conditions. After that, Tierra is on its own. Once it is running, Ray observes that Tierra forms two primary evolutionary strategies to best capture the system's two main resources—compute time (energy) and memory (space). The first strategy is organisms that evolve synergistically, the second is organisms that evolve solely to replicate faster, fill-

6. Ibid., section The Metaphor.

ing up the soup with their own kind. In both cases, Ray's system displays evolving genetic structure, interaction between the organisms, and natural selection. In other words, Tierra contains all the necessary features of an evolving world; it is a nascent digital ecology.

From the beginning, Ray understood that staying out of the way of his system's process was the best strategy for achieving digital evolution. From his years as an ecologist, he brought to the medium a deep respect for the power of evolution. Ray knew that it would do a much better job of reaching the goal of increased complexity than he ever could. Again and again during the developers' conference, people would present often quite complex "what if" scenarios. Ray's answer was always, We don't know; we will have to run the program and see what happens. Ray is extremely reluctant to shape the environment any more than he has to. As a result, his approach is resolutely not reductionist. His approach is *synthetic*. Ray is "building life rather than taking it apart."[7]

In addition to his hands-off philosophy, Ray brings to the digital medium an inherent respect for what it is, not what we need or want it to be. This respect can be felt in the way he calls the evolving bits of code "organisms," a nod to their lifelike behavior. Central to his philosophy in creating Tierra is the desire to understand what evolution might feel like from the organisms' perspective. In other words, he puts himself into the medium, trying to extract and understand its essential features. This stance may well be why he has had such rapid and early success in his efforts. As he writes, "Evolution is a process that explores the possibilities inherent in the medium in which it is embedded."[8] Therefore, to get evolution going, one has to understand the substrate one is working in.

---

7. Ibid., section Synthetic Evolution.

8. Ibid., section Evolution and the Medium.

As Ray explains, the digital world is a "logical informational universe."[9] In this universe, the primary "physics" on which evolution builds are the operating system, the memory space, the logic of the processor, and the clock cycle of the central processing unit. Because the evolving organisms live in the RAM software, space in the terms that Euclid described it means nothing to them. Ray claims that people often think that the "space" inside a computer is one-dimensional, a flat grid of numbers assigned to certain memory locations. But from the digital perspective, there is no concept of linear distance. There is no such thing as a line between two points in cyberspace, any more than there is a numerically defined line between two ideas in our minds. Ray argues that the most useful "analog of distance is the time it takes to move information between points. Thus time becomes the metric for distance in memory space."[10] Life for digital organisms is pure process stripped of any of the messy and confusing physical complexity that masks the underlying processes of evolution from view in our daily lives. Systems like Tierra could open up a whole new way of thinking about the power of process and evolutionary creativity in our lives.

GOD ENTERS FROM THE BOTTOM UP

It is often said that those men and women who are trying to coax intelligence out of the digital medium are playing God games. In many papers written about artificial intelligence and A-life, there are brief

---

9. Ibid.
10. Ibid.

sections detailing the rules that mortal Gods must follow. These include various features such as killing organisms, designing the ways in which they reproduce, selecting goals for them to achieve, and even initiating apocalypse functions that wipe out whole populations. The appellation "God" is used facetiously at best. But to take it seriously for a moment, one must ask, What are these men and women doing when they play God? They are attempting to create intelligence and/or life in the digital. This is a powerful goal with enormous implications. In this context, the kind of God one tries to be matters enormously. The history of artificial intelligence (AI) mirrors two distinctly different God-like attempts, each of which reflects a deeper theological premise.

The discipline of artificial intelligence has been trying for more than twenty-five years to develop intelligence in the digital medium. In the last decade, this science has split into two factions—those who believe we can engineer intelligence once we know enough about it, and those who believe that it must grow organically, from the ground up. These two approaches reflect two different value sets. In the first instance, there is a strong materialist and reductionist bias that argues that our own intelligence can ultimately be picked apart into its constituent pieces, coded in digital form, and then rebuilt inside a computer. This approach is often known as "top-down programming."[11] Its methodology attempts to create intelligence in machines through a predefined set of programming rules. Over the years, this methodology has produced many vast and complex software schematics that have been

---

11. This methodology is also called "good old artificial intelligence." There is some debate within the field of AI about the terminology of top-down versus bottom-up. Naturally, many scientists use a mixture of both approaches to build their systems. But, in general, one can divide the field into these two broad camps, with many falling roughly into one side or the other.

painstakingly turned into strings of code in hopes of building intelligent systems.

In theological terms, one could say that the top-down programmers are playing the role of the traditional, Judeo-Christian father God who brings forth life through divine omnipotence. This is the God who knows all things, sees all things, and controls all things from his[12] transcendent perch. In order to affect the world, this God must make the choice to break into his creation and manipulate it. This God does not naturally participate in the ongoing creativity of the creatures of the universe. Any divine participation for this God takes the form of divine intervention.

In the late 1980s, a new AI methodology began to become popular. Known as "bottom-up" programming, or emergent computation, this approach relies on a series of independent software "agents" that interact with one another to produce results. There is a wide range of approaches contained in bottom-up AI, but all of them share the fundamental tenet of which Ray's work with evolutionary systems serves as an excellent example—relinquish control. As Kevin Kelly writes, "When everything is connected to everything in a distributed network, everything happens at once. When everything happens at once, wide and fast-moving problems simply route around any central authority. Therefore overall governance must arise from the most humble acts done locally in parallel, not from a central command."[13] As in an ant colony, complex behavior emerges from lots of small organisms working in parallel, not from some grand design implemented from above.

Bottom-up programming, or emergent computation, is defined as a

---

12. I use the masculine deliberately in this case. This God is very much a God the Father.

13. Kevin Kelly, *Out of Control,* page 469.

computational system wherein both the explicit programming and the emergent phenomena are computations. The fact that emergence takes the form of computation in these systems does not mean, however, that its inherent mystery has disappeared. Emergence—the ability of something to be greater than the sum of its parts—is a universal phenomenon found in many substrates. What is fascinating and important for our examination is that this mysterious, ultimately divine force is now making itself felt in the world of cyberspace.

In the relatively simple instances we have of emergent computation, the *product* of the emergent process can be mapped. The printouts will reveal the way, for example, that Deep Blue considered its moves before arriving at its brilliant strategy or the moment when the organisms began to reproduce. But the printouts are after the fact. The process itself, why the emergence happened, remains largely mysterious. Many computer researchers[14] agree that in the case of highly complex systems such as the human brain, it is actually impossible to determine a formal description of the emergent level. In other words, the emergent level cannot be reduced to formulae; it is born of process. This is precisely the power of the bottom-up method.

Stephanie Forrest, in the introduction to her volume *Emergent Computation,* lists the requirements for emergent computation as follows: "A collection of agents, each following explicit instructions; interactions among the agents (according to the instructions), which form implicit global patterns at the macroscopic level, i.e., epiphenom-

---

14. Stephanie Forrest, on page 3 of *Emergent Computation,* cites the following articles as examples of this argument: D. R. Hofstadter, "Artificial Intelligence: Subcognition as Computation," *Technical Report* 132, Indiana University, Bloomington, IN, 1982; C. G. Langton, ed., *Artificial Life,* Santa Fe Institute Studies in the Sciences of Complexity, Addison-Wesley, Reading, MA, 1989; E. N. Lorenz, "Deterministic Nonperiodic Flow," *Journal of Atmospheric Science* 20, 1963, pages 130–41; and R. Shaw, "Strange Attractors, Chaotic Behavior, and Information Flow," *Z. Naturforsch* 36a, 1981, pages 80–112.

ena; a natural interpretation of the epiphenomena as computations."[15] The explicit instructions can be thought of as the mechanistic aspect of the system. These form the "physics" of the system, the objective aspects of the information, to use Jahn's term, or the radial energy, to recall Teilhard. On the basis of these interactions, implicit or subjective epiphenomena emerge. In the case of Tierra, these are the evolutionary processes that the system displays.

Tierra is an example of almost pure bottom-up programming. Tierra's abilities to mutate and to create emergent fitness in its organisms are its greatest strengths. However, achieving more complex results such as "multicellular" organisms has remained elusive. At this point, it is unclear how much computer power and time may be required to reach this level of complexity. But Ray is a purist and is unwilling to impose too much control on the nascent evolutionary processes. He wants digital complexity if and when it comes from within the system as a truly emergent phenomenon.

Other bottom-up programmers set external goals for the system that guide it in certain directions. The best example of this is a class of programming techniques called genetic programming, or GPs. GP systems are designed to search large information spaces for specific solutions. From the outset, the system designer establishes some predefined "fitness function" or goal. How the system reaches the goal is not determined. The system gets there any way that it can, using evolution as the motor. In GP systems, strings of code are organized in treelike hierarchies. Any node in any tree can mutate and cross over and thereby share genetic information with any other tree. The GP is an example of directed evolution, or using the power of evolution to achieve specific goals.

---

15. Stephanie Forrest, *Emergent Computation,* page 2.

One potent example of a GP system can be found in the work of Karl Sims, an artificial-intelligence pioneer. Sims uses a unique set of "fitness functions" based on very high-level variables. In one system, he presents the user with a variety of computer-generated images. The user then selects his or her favorite two images. The system then "breeds" these two images together to create a new set of images. The process is repeated again and again until the user reaches a pleasing picture. Sims calls this process "aesthetic selection." In another example, Sims creates a population of creatures each of which is constructed from a collection of "blocks" linked by flexible joints. He then puts these creatures in an environment that simulates something in the real world, such as water. The creatures are then selected according to a set of fitness functions such as ability to swim, to swim in a particular direction, and so on. The results look a lot like the evolution of the first multicelled creatures—a wild diversity of solutions, some of which are familiar and others that are quite unlike anything we have ever seen before.

On the other end of the spectrum are examples of self-organization that happen purely spontaneously in systems where not only do we not expect them, but where they can create real problems. Stephanie Forrest cites the following example: "The Internet was designed so that messages would be routed somewhat randomly (there are usually many different routes that a message may take between two Internet hosts). The intent is for message traffic to be evenly distributed across various hosts. However, in some circumstances the messages have been found to self-organize into a higher-level structure, called a token-passing ring, so that all of the messages collect at one node in the ring. In this case, the self-organization is highly detrimental to the overall performance of the network."[16] Cases like this can cause logjams in the flow of informa-

---

16. Ibid., page 8.

tion moving around the Net, resulting in sluggish system performance. Self-organization is the through-line that binds all of these examples, from Tierra to Internet logjams, together. And self-organization, as earlier chapters have spelled out, is born from a powerful mix of objective and subjective, radial and tangential forces. In other words, wherever self-organization is in evidence, the power of divine creativity is active. As these examples show, this force is now engaging the digital terrain. With this potent fact in mind, we can look once again at those men and women who practice bottom-up design. These people are playing God games of a very different sort.

Novelty, a key concept in thinking about self-organization, is a slippery term. Its definition can vary widely according to one's point of view. Is something novel when we have never seen it before—in other words, from our perspective? Or is something novel from the perspective of the phenomenon in question? This issue becomes particularly important when dealing with computational emergence. We have a tendency to explain away computational novelty because we can look back at the digital record and see how it happened. We tell ourselves that no matter how complex the resulting computation, it is still a string of code. There is no inherent mystery there, no element that makes the whole greater than the sum of its parts. No mystery, no emergence, no novelty. Artificial-intelligence pioneer Marvin Minsky calls this the "disappearing AI problem." As AI researcher Pattie Maes explains, "We call something intelligent when we don't know how it is done. But as soon as we understand how it works, as soon as it is made trivial that way, we don't consider it intelligent anymore. So that's why we call it the disappearing AI problem. As soon as AI makes a contribution, people say, 'Oh that's just a program.' In the same vein, we can say, 'Oh, that's just computational emergence. It's not real emergence, it doesn't represent real novelty.' "

Why not? In computational emergence, it is an unavoidable fact that *events* are produced that are more than the sum of their parts. This is an important distinction. The novelty is found in the events taking place in the system, not in the strings of code to which those events can be reduced. It is the *process* of self-organization that is novel, not the products of that event, such as the algorithms. Computational *emergence* represents novelty in a new guise, acting in a new substrate, but it is novelty nonetheless.

With computational emergence and self-organization, we find divinity present in the digital. In this medium, it makes sense that the divine expresses itself in the form of digital strings. What is remarkable, and truly awesome, is that when numbers of these small, simple digital strings are thrown together and left to run, lifelike properties emerge entirely independently. Nonlinear systems are born—networks, populations, swarms, and colonies. It can be no accident that these baby systems reflect the same processes that we see in the organic world. There is a through-line between carbon and silicon, between the digital and the analog. Both realms are born of the same confluence of physics, chemistry, and divine creativity.

GODS OF PERSUASION

An explanation of how the universe came to be can be found in every religious tradition. In the Judeo-Christian tradition, the meaning of the creation story is endlessly debated. The majority of the interpretations have sided with the primary explanation of *creatio ex nihilo,* or creation from nothing. Many people who embrace this view believe in

God the King, the omnipotent God, or what theologian David Griffin calls the "God of coercion." This notion, which found a powerful voice in the writings of Augustine, claims that because God created the world from nothing, God remains absolutely powerful and therefore absolutely free in relation to the world. It follows then that God's relation to the world is purely voluntary. As Griffin writes, "The voluntarists . . . portrayed God not as being itself which was immanent throughout creation, but as *a* being, an individual, who existed outside the world. The world existed not through participation but through an external act of creation, which was entirely voluntary. The nature of the world's relation to God, and even the fact a world exists at all, were in no way natural or 'given' features of reality."[17]

The idea of creation from nothing and its attendant voluntary God poses an enormous number of problems. How can a God, whom we claim as purely good, but who is also absolutely powerful, allow evil to exist in the world? This trenchant problem has probably created more contemporary atheists than any other theological issue. It just doesn't make sense. But in process theology, the issue is examined from a very different perspective. God, for process theologians, is the principle that brings order from chaos, not that creates something from nothing. As Whitehead wrote, "the creation of the world is the incoming of a type of order establishing a cosmic epoch. It is not the beginning of matter of fact, but the incoming of a certain type of social order."[18]

As David Griffin explains, this understanding is a natural outcome of Whitehead's epistemology. For Whitehead, the world is composed of an endless series of creative events. Recall that for each event, "The many become one and are increased by one." In other words, each

---

17. David Ray Griffin, *God & Religion in the Postmodern World,* page 130.
18. Ibid., page 138.

event begins with an infinite array of influences that it takes and forms into a unity of experience. The event then exerts a creative influence on subsequent events. This is the evolutionary process. Within this process, creativity is the ultimate reality that is embodied both by God and the rest of creation. But, as each event has its own free will, its own "power of self-creation,"[19] God can never be omnipotent. Rather, God is the ultimate actuality that lures every other actuality toward goodness, truth, beauty, and peace. But in each instance, each actuality is free to choose otherwise. David Griffin writes, "It is through the steady divine persuasion that order has been coaxed out of chaos and that the higher forms of existence, which make possible the higher forms of value, have come into being."[20]

The God that coaxes order from chaos is quite different from the God that creates from nothing. The former is the *God of persuasion,* the God that is omniscient, but not omnipotent. This God is the force that ushers chaos into ever greater form and order through the continual introduction of novelty. The relationship between this God and the world rests not on God's volition but is "founded upon the necessities of the nature of God and the nature of the world."[21] In other words, the God of persuasion, through God's very nature, is infused throughout the whole of the universe. This divinity influences the world but does not control it absolutely. Each individual is free to choose either with the divine or against it. Either way, the choices of the individuals, which remain related to but distinct from God, influence the divine as well. Contained in this understanding is the basic truth that the divine influences us and we influence the divine in an endless dance of becoming.

19. Ibid., page 42.

20. Ibid., page 43.

21. As quoted in ibid., page 138.

Some people are horrified when they hear the notion of a God of persuasion, a divinity that is not omnipotent. How, they wonder, can one have faith in a power that is not supreme? John Cobb offers an elegant response to this issue when he explains, "If God is omnipotent, then nothing else has any power. That is the strict meaning of omnipotence. How significant is the power that is exercised over the totally powerless thing? Significant power is power which empowers or frees other things. This understanding signifies a basic shift in the way in which we understand power. The more power there is in creation, the more power there is in God. It's not true that the more power God has, the less power we have. And obviously that is the way love operates. The more love people have, the more they are able to love others."

When power is distributed throughout creation, the whole, including God, becomes more powerful. But this can happen only when self-determination and freedom are also distributed throughout creation. The God of coercion creates a world filled with automata, zombies fulfilling their programming. Indeed, certain well-respected philosophers—gurus of top-down AI approaches, such as Daniel Dennet, author of *Consciousness Explained*—believe just that. We are nothing but zombies, programmed not by God but by our genes. It is interesting to note that absolute materialists, such as Dennet, have much in common philosophically with absolute deists. The primary cause may be different, God versus genetic code, but the outcome is much the same. We ultimately have no power to choose good or evil; we are simply responding to our natural or supernatural programming.

Bottom-up programmers are playing the games of Gods of persuasion. In their work, they set parameters, influence the worlds they are building, but then they step back in such a way that the creatures can express their own self-determination and freedom. This approach is proving to be a powerful way to create complex, nonlinear systems. As

Stephanie Forrest writes, "For [intelligent systems], it is impossible to get enough flexibility from explicit instructions; for realistic environments, it is just not possible to program all contingencies ahead of time. Therefore, the flexibility must appear at the emergent level."[22] It should come as no surprise that with the bottom-up approach, evolution has begun to emerge in the digital. The true God of persuasion, working through the mortal gods of persuasion, is a powerful lure for novelty.

The physicist Paul Davies sums up the issue beautifully when he writes, "Central to Whitehead's philosophy is that God is responsible for ordering the world, not through direct action, but by providing the various potentialities which the physical universe is then free to actualize. In this way, God does not compromise the essential openness and indeterminism of the universe, but is nevertheless in a position to encourage a trend toward good. Traces of this subtle and indirect influence may be discerned in the progressive nature of biological evolution, for example, and the tendency of the universe to self-organize into a richer variety of ever more complex forms. Whitehead thus replaces the monarchical image of God as omnipotent creator and ruler to that of a participator in the creative process. He is no longer self-sufficient and unchanging, but influences, and is influenced by, the unfolding reality of the physical universe."[23]

Perhaps we are meant to be Gods of persuasion, consciously participating in the evolutionary process. After all, we are, as Teilhard pointed out, evolution become aware of itself. In this sense, our role is complex, multidimensional, and still very much working itself out. Our inherited notion that the universe is ruled by an omnipotent father God may no longer work for us as we seek to blend the digital world into

---

22. Stephanie Forrest, *Emergent Computation,* page 3.
23. Paul Davies, *The Mind of God,* page 183.

our own. The truth is that we cannot control cyberspace any more than God controls us. As Kevin Kelly writes of those who play God games, "To succeed at all in creating a creative creature, the creators have to turn over control to the created, just has Yahweh relinquished control to them. To be a god, at least to be a creative one, one must relinquish control and embrace uncertainty. Absolute control is absolutely boring. To birth the new, the unexpected, the truly novel—that is, to be genuinely surprised—one must surrender the seat of power to the mob below. The great irony of god games is that letting go is the only way to win."[24]

THE APPEARANCE OF THE COLLECTIVE

Pattie Maes, an artificial-intelligence guru at MIT's Media Lab, wears a computer everywhere she goes. At the Media Lab, an advanced research facility geared to developing creative, real-world applications of technology, such experiments are commonplace. The Remembrance Agent, one of many projects being undertaken at the Autonomous Agents Group at the Media Lab, consists of a small computer equipped with a general positioning system (GPS). The computer logs everything that goes on in a person's life by time, place, and recorded samples of sound. Records can then be searched either by keywords or by a description of a certain event. When is the last time I had my keys? What was the name of the person I ran into on the way to the subway? The Remembrance Agent is just one example of what Pattie Maes calls "augmented intelligence."

---

24. Kevin Kelly, *Out of Control*, page 257.

Maes did not arrive at the idea of augmented intelligence overnight. For many years she worked with Marvin Minsky, one of the great founding figures of AI. Minsky's goal has always closely paralleled that of traditional AI—to figure out how our intelligence works, load it into a machine, and create an intelligent being. When Maes shifted from the AI Lab to the Media Lab, a research facility concerned primarily with human/computer interaction, it slowly became clear that computing could serve a much more powerful role by doing what it does best and augmenting what we do best. As Maes explains, echoing Tom Ray, "I don't believe that there is just one kind of intelligence. If we do build intelligent machines, the nature of that intelligence will be very different from our own. It won't shed much light on the nature of our own intelligence. What is much more interesting to me now is the idea of augmenting people's intelligence through computation, because I think computer intelligence and human intelligence are different and complementary."

With this idea foremost in mind, Maes and her colleagues at the Media Lab have developed a host of applications based on what is known as autonomous agents. These simple strings of software, embedded in complex, unpredictable environments, are capable of perceiving, adapting, and communicating to one another and to us in highly sophisticated ways. In this research, the force of self-organization is being marshaled to create a collective that will have profound implications for the future of the human/computer relationship. This relationship will be based fundamentally on nonmechanistic, unpredictable, and spontaneous behavior.

Maes begins with a very different goal from that of Tom Ray. Her approach is more pragmatic. She is interested in creating a new paradigm for how people interact with their computers. As Maes explains, "Today, the nature of a computer and how we use it is completely dif-

ferent. The computer is no longer a closed system. Instead, it is a window onto a vast and dynamic world of people and information that is
constantly changing and completely unstructured. The metaphor of one
person being in control doesn't apply anymore. . . . Alan Kay is the one
who came up with the term *indirect management*—meaning that
instead of directly manipulating visual representations of objects, you
delegate tasks and roles to agents that know what you are interested in
and how you want things done, and that can act on your behalf."[25] For
example, you might use an agent to search the Net for you, finding the
best price on a certain item, locating a long-lost friend, or retrieving
articles on a given topic.

The agents that Maes creates are traditional bottom-up organisms.
They are quite simple individually, but when let loose in an environment, assigned specific goals, and allowed to evolve, they begin to display complex and creative behavior. This behavior arises in part
because there are whole populations of agents working on the same
goals. They work collaboratively, sharing information and learning
from one another. They also evolve. For example, in one system, Maes's
group evolved agents whose goal was to suggest to a user Web pages to
visit. When the agents suggested Web pages the user liked, they would
be assigned a higher fitness rating than those that suggested pages the
user wasn't interested in. Those with a higher rating would be selected
to reproduce more quickly.

From our perspective, these systems appear to be intelligent. They
adapt, they problem-solve, they learn. They are, in a word, creative.
The primary feature that enables this behavior is what Maes calls a
"generative" approach to creativity. There is an almost infinite number of routes to the assigned goal, and the agents are free to choose

---

25. Pattie Maes, "You Light Up My Life," *The Red Herring,* December 1996, page 35.

among them. In other words, the agents tap into the power of self-organization and evolution, generating their own novelty. As Maes writes, "Although they are still primitive, [these] artificial-life agents are truly autonomous: in effect, they program themselves. Their software is designed to change its behavior based on experience and interactions with other agents."[26]

The MIT group has designed a wide variety of systems based on proactive, adaptive, and personalized agents. These include those designed to help us cope with the increasing amount of information in our lives, such as agents that search the Internet for interesting or appropriate Web pages, news articles, or music, video, movie, and restaurant suggestions; personalized e-mail and calendar agents that organize and prioritize mail and appointments; and a Usenet agent that sorts through the massive postings in newsgroups to find nuggets of interest. For example, in Firefly, a system that Maes has launched as a privately held company, agents help to automate "word of mouth" communication. The user rates his or her tastes in movies or music, then the agent compares this to the tastes of other users in the system, determining the user's "nearest neighbors." With this information, the agent makes suggestions about new music or movies the user might want to try. The more the user "trains" the agent, and the more people enter the system, the more accurate the agent will be. This is a truly synergistic approach to human/computer interaction.

Another interesting implementation of autonomous agents is the Yenta system designed by Maes and Leonard Foner. In this system, the agent is trained to find and introduce people with matching interests who have never met one another. It is important to note that Yenta is

26. Pattie Maes, "Intelligent Software," page 3, available at:
http://pattie.www.media.mit.edu/people/pattie/SciAm-95.html

also concerned with the very real problem of privacy and agents. As the authors write, "The project is an experiment in creating a decentralized, fault-tolerant application that handles potentially sensitive information (such as people's mail, their personal files, or lists of their particular interests) in a responsible and privacy-protecting fashion, using cryptographic and other techniques."[27] In a similar vein is Kasbah, designed by Maes and Anthony Chavez, an agent marketplace for buying and selling goods. This system proactively seeks out buyers and sellers and negotiates with them on the user's behalf. These systems, and others like them, treat the complexity of the human environment on the Internet as an asset to be explored creatively.

All of these systems share a handful of common attributes that are worth noting. The systems are built on decentralized, distributed architectures. Each agent in the system is an "expert" in one small area of competence and communicates with the environment and other agents through a series of simple messages, sensors, and effectors. The systems contain no hierarchical, central control mechanisms. The complex behavior that emerges from the decentralized architecture comes from "feedback loops" located "between the agent and the environment, between the different modules inside the agent and between multiple agents."[28] Last, the architecture contains much redundancy to ensure a high level of fault tolerance and to encourage "non-mechanistic behavior."[29]

What all of this means in plain English is that the autonomy and

27. Leonard Foner, "Yenta—Matchmaking Agents," available at:
http://lcs.www.media.mit.edu/groups/agents

28. Pattie Maes, "Artificial Life Meets Entertainment: Lifelike Autonomous Agents,"
available at:
http://pattie.www.media.mit.edu/people/pattie/CACM-95/alife-cacm95.html

29. Ibid.

complexity Maes's agents demonstrate depend on many levels of cooperative behavior and feedback. In these systems, everything is linked to everything else in a vast, dynamic web. Cooperation, it turns out, is a basic feature of self-organizing systems. Stephanie Forrest points out that there are actually two kinds of cooperation in a computational setting. The first she calls "program correctness." This refers to the fact that adaptation takes place at the level of the instructions or the agent, but the cooperative behavior appears at the level of the collective or the system. The second meaning has to do with shared resources. There are many examples of agent systems learning to share both internal and external resources ranging from CPU time to printers in a very robust way. In both cases, the cooperative behavior is an emergent property, observable at the level of the collective.

The emergent cooperation that these bottom-up systems gravitate toward reflects a larger pattern inherent in the dynamic of divine creativity active in the universe. In order to shed some light on this important connection, we return once again to the work of John Cobb. Recall that the fundamental tenet of process thinking is the interrelationship of all things, living and nonliving, in a vast web of life. In this view, objects are defined by their participation in their environment, not by their individual essence. In fact, they have no individual essence separate from their field of experience. "Events are primary, and substantial objects are to be viewed as enduring patterns among changing events. . . . The event is a synthesis of relations to other events."[30] Cobb calls this view "event thinking." Metaphysically grounded in a philosophy of holism, event thinking is relational. It rejects mechanistic, atomistic, dualistic thinking as partial and incomplete.

Event thinking implies that all things are related *internally*. Sub-

---

30. Charles Birch and John Cobb, *The Liberation of Life,* page 95.

stance thinking, the term Birch and Cobb use to refer to the current mechanistic norm, sees things as related only externally. In other words, in the substance view, things are affected only if an external force is placed on them by another substance. Event thinking turns this idea inside out as it posits that things are defined by their internal relations. "For example," writes Cobb, "field theory in physics shows that the events which make up the field have their existence only as parts of the field. These events cannot exist apart from the field. They are internally related to one another."[31]

This idea is somewhat difficult to grasp when we retain a desire to see in our mind's eye a web of "stuff" weaving all things together. Internal relations are not based on any "stuff," but rather on process itself. It is the processes, the field of events, that tie everything into one vast whole in the web of creation. This is why, as Stephanie Forrest pointed out earlier, emergent behavior is apparent only at the level of the whole system or the collective. As Birch and Cobb write, "There is no way to go below the level of the systematic interconnections of events to another level at which there are self-contained entities whose properties in isolation from each other explain the system."[32] Bottom-up software systems serve as powerful examples of this truth.

The implications of internal relations require that we add another dimension to the evolutionary ideas of chance and necessity. When faced with emergent behavior, the factor of context must be added to the picture. As a simple example, imagine two seeds from the same pine tree. The first drops from the parent and takes root in an established ecosystem. Finding close to ideal conditions for its growth, this tree achieves the fullest expression its genetic code will allow. The second

---

31. Ibid., page 88.
32. Ibid., page 83.

seed is eaten by a bird and dropped many miles away on a bare and scrubby hillside. It too takes root, but throughout its short life it remains stunted and deformed. The distinctive factor in these two cases is the environment in which the seed sprouted.

The environment or context forms a crucial factor in the world of digital agents. In fact, as Maes's work recognizes, agents are to a large degree defined by their environment. As they adapt, learn, and evolve, they alter their environment. In the next time step, what they have to adapt to is different once again. The same dynamic is true for collectives of digital agents. The learning and adaptation of the other agents is a fundamental part of their own evolution. This cooperative behavior appears to be such a fundamental feature of the universe that it emerges in digital systems even when it wasn't selected for, programmed, or expected. As Tom Ray writes, "The first evolution observed in Tierra was the origin of ecological interactions, which were based on adaptation to the presence of other digital organisms in the environment."[33]

Ecological interactions, or internal relations, are processes or events unfolding in time. This is true in any system, whether it be as small as Tierra or as large as the cosmos. The primary stuff of interrelatedness—whether between agents and their environment, humans and cyberspace, or humans and humans—is the processes in which we participate. This fundamental truth may be more obvious in the digital terrain than it is in our own world.

Within these processes, the divine force of creativity forms the primary glue that holds the whole together. Without creative leaps and the lure toward ever richer experience that the divine provides, we would

---

33. Tom Ray, "Artificial Life," section Auto-catalytic Evolution, available at: http://www.hip.atr.co.jp/~ray/pubs/fatm/fatm.html

be locked into endlessly repeating cycles of stasis. Clearly, this is not the nature of reality. The universe, on every level, is a vast whole woven together with physics, chemistry, evolution, and spirit. The emergent behaviors we can observe in these nascent digital systems are not aberrations; they are reflections of the larger reality in which we are all embedded.

The work being undertaken by digital pioneers such as Tom Ray and Patty Maes may or may not lead to the development of complex, digital intelligences. In the end we are not Gods. As history has shown, our efforts to act as stewards for the life around us have been fairly dismal. We are, at best, poor handmaidens for the evolutionary process, learning in small, incremental steps. And yet, whether or not they create genuine intelligence or full-blown life in cyberspace may not matter. What Ray and Maes have shown us is that even with our current technology, evolution and self-organization can occur in the digital medium. This reality serves as a wake-up call whispering that divine presence is now being felt in a world very different from and yet utterly woven throughout our own. This divine presence requires us to redirect our attention and attitudes toward the cyberworld. A prayerful attitude of respect, not unlike what we might direct to the plants of the forest or the waves that crash on earth's shores, may be in order. This attitude could well be accompanied by a feeling of gratitude for the wonders of divine power and persistence—a power than can envelop even such a seemingly stark, dead medium. The piece of sacred creation of which we are aware has expanded once again.

(7)

BLURRING THE
BOUNDARIES

I breathe in and float upward, passing through shimmering globes and layers of ephemeral, earth-tone patterns. I lean left and drift through a dreamlike leaf world, chasing receding balls of light. As I drift, ethereal voices float around my ears, melodic and yet indistinct male and female songs that respond to my movements. I exhale and sink into the trunk of a vast tree set amid a large clearing. The interior of the tree glows with an odd luminescence as I follow channels of light-infused sap, flying through its depths merely by leaning my body and breathing.

I am inside Osmose, Char Davies's virtual reality artwork. This unusual application of computer technology delivers me into a dreamscape where my logical faculties melt into a deep, meditative awareness centered in my breath and body. As I breathe in, I float up in the world; as I exhale, I float down. Davies achieves this simple and yet utterly unique technique for navigating virtual space through the use of a chest harness that monitors my breath. This harness includes a breathing and balance sensor that tracks my body's movement in real time. When combined with the 3-D VR helmet I wear on my head and fat cables linking the whole to a high-powered, parallel-processing Silicon Graphics Onyx computer, I become immersed in cyberspace in a way that explodes my previous conceptions of the medium.

I am not alone in this reaction. A consensus has emerged among those who have experienced immersion in Osmose that it inspires feelings of deep peace and reverie, inducing a quasi-meditative state of awareness. Immersants, as Davies calls them, speak of feeling connected to themselves and the world in a new way after a journey through Osmose. Media theorist Brenda Laurel calls Osmose "breathtaking" and comments that it is "a fundamentally powerful use of technology in the service of, dare I say, nature. There's a healing there, not just of individuals, but of the technology itself."[1]

This healing is precisely Davies's goal. Cyberspace, in its current manifestation, has a tendency to further the split between our minds and our bodies. We enter it through a flat, two-dimensional screen and engage it primarily with our minds, leaving our bodies, for the most part, behind. In fact, for many cyber-aficionados, the body in the context of cyberspace is reduced to "meat," a characterization that denigrates and minimizes the profound power of physical experience.

As Davies's work demonstrates, the radical objectification of the body in the context of cyberspace is not an inevitability produced by the medium itself. Instead, as Sherry Turkle's[2] work amply demonstrates, cyberspace acts as a mirror that reflects a wide variety of cul-

---

1. Erik Davis, "Osmose," available at:
   http://www.wired.com/wired/4.08/features/osmose.html
2. See Sherry Turkle, *Life on the Screen* and *The Second Self.*

tural needs and conditions. When it comes to our bodies, cyberspace reflects our entrenched habit of splitting our minds and bodies, thereby reducing the primal power of our physical selves.

This well-documented cultural trajectory, also known as the "mind-body split," has had devastating consequences in severing not only our minds from our bodies but also humanity from the earth that we inhabit. From our split stance, we have sought to objectify and control the physical world, reducing nature to a complex of resources to be plundered at will. This attitude has not only contributed to environmental degradation at an alarming rate but has almost wholly excised the physical from our sacred reality, casting us adrift in an objectified world.

Viewed through windows, menus, and icons, cyberspace seems the perfect bedfellow for our disembodied reveries. But this interpretation reflects our reality, not the reality of cyberspace itself. If we approach cyberspace from the perspective of a splintered self, we will re-create this dualism in cyberspace. If, however, we see cyberspace as a part of a larger, integrated, sacred experience of the world, the picture begins to change quite dramatically. Artists such as Davies are beginning to break through into new experiences of cyberspace that are guided by deeply felt, sacred, and holistic understandings of the world and our role in it.

BODILY WISDOM

The first time I was immersed in Osmose, I came to the environment with a heightened sense of my physicality—I was almost six months pregnant with my second son. For me, pregnancy is a time of deep, physical awareness, much of it unpleasant. At six months, I was still experiencing fatigue and nausea. In this light, the ability of Osmose to engage my body in a new way was a welcome change. As in meditation, my focus shifted to my breath, centered and grounded in my body. Through my breath, my body became a source of calm. I found myself falling slowly into a state of reverie tinged with delight as I drifted through Osmose with my baby kicking inside my swelling belly. In the session, time collapsed, and I was shocked to find when I came out that I had been immersed for forty-five minutes, an unusually long time.

While in Osmose, I found that my analytic sensibility dissolved as I floated among its various worlds. When I first entered the environment, I saw a three-dimensional, phosphorescent green grid against a black background. This "Cartesian" grid quickly faded as I entered the "clearing," a dim space suffused with filtered light. As my eyes adjusted, I saw in the middle of the clearing a majestic tree standing in front of a pool of water. I leaned forward and moved toward the tree. As I got closer, I entered the tree and then, going deeper, moved into its leaves. As I exhaled, I sank into the root system of the tree, entering a space that had a profound earthy quality. Again I leaned forward and found myself back in the clearing. I saw a trail of small lights, like fireflies, floating away in the distance. I followed them lazily, moving among the leaf world, the tree, the clearing, and the cloud world above. At one point, I sank into a pond at the foot of the tree, entering what Davies calls the "abyss," a world of seemingly infinite space in which floated a shimmering ball. As I moved toward the ball and entered it, I found myself back in the clearing once again, a neat circularity that further short-circuited my ability to create a linear experience of the space.

Once I became accustomed to the general parameters of Osmose, I tried to float upward as far as I could. To my surprise, I found beyond the clouds the "text" world, a space of floating words. Generally a person deeply tantalized by evocative and poetic phrases, I quickly grew impatient in this world. My intellect had shut off and I wasn't ready to reengage it. I exhaled and sank down through the clouds, the clearing, and the earth until I found myself in another world of text floating on a black background. This was the "code" world and was composed of all the software code Osmose employs to generate its images. In this world I became deeply anxious. I didn't want to be in the code. I wanted to be back in the archetypal images of nature. Responding to my emotional state, I focused all my attention on rising to escape the floating, numeric sequences.

My experience in Osmose threw me back on myself, gently prodding new awarenesses to the surface. I noticed that I was deeply comfortable in the most ambiguous of the spaces—the transitions among the various worlds. When each world became clearly recognizable—as tree, leaf, or pond—the luminous quality of the floating lights receded into the background. At that point, I began to interpret and distance myself from my immediate experience. My response was to return to the transitional spaces where the images and the sounds floated around me in an indistinct yet beautiful and soothing way. I also found my antipathy to the text world and my deep anxiety in the code world fascinating. These were unexpected responses generated from deep in my psyche, responses that seemed to escape my interpretive abilities.

In the hours following my immersion, images of Osmose continued to surface in my mind's eye. At one point, I was powerfully reminded of a passage I had recently read in a book by Stuart Kauffman, a scientist at the Santa Fe Institute. Kauffman's book, *At Home in the Universe,* explores his thesis that the emergence of life can be scientifically explained through the study of self-organizing systems. Kauffman believes that life is, for a variety of complex reasons, an inevitability in the trajectory of evolution. In a passage early in the book, describing the gestation of a human embryo, he writes, "the magic of ontogony lies in the fact that genes and their RNA and protein products form a complex network, switching one another on and off in a wondrously precise manner."[3]

As I was reminded of the passage, I suddenly understood it in a new light. Life, I thought, is emerging in my belly right at this moment and the magic is much larger than my genes and RNA. There is magic in the peace I feel and the visceral sense that that peace is connected, in some deep way, to the peace women have felt for thousands of years as they gestate their children. This is a bodily magic beyond my RNA that is related to the fact that growing inside me is a sliver of myself joined with a sliver of another person, my husband. Through the experience of gestation, I feel both my uniqueness and, at the same time, how deeply connected I am to the greater whole of human evolution.

The deep sense of interdependence that I felt so powerfully flies in the face of evolutionary theory. In the world of traditional evolutionary science, sex is a puzzle. If evolution proceeds through natural selection, through survival of the fittest, then an act that relies on two individuals each cooperatively contributing a piece of genetic material doesn't make sense. In a world strictly guided by competition, evolution would logically create ways for each individual to selfishly pass on his or her genes in a dominant way. Why, evolutionary theory asks, did sex evolve as a solution for reproduction? The answer seems clear enough to me.

The experience in my body tells me that sexual union leading to new life creates a deep awareness of cooperation and interdependence, linking me inextricably into a larger whole. But why does this confer an evolutionary advantage? It doesn't necessarily, until one considers the telos of evolution, its hidden, spiritual core. From a sacred perspective, evolution has a purpose, a direction, toward greater unity that is just as much a part of its reality as is natural selection. The Judeo-Christian

---

3. Stuart Kauffman, *At Home in the Universe,* pages 24–25.

tradition identifies this evolutionary trajectory as toward greater unity through love. This is what Cobb and Griffin refer to when they speak of the subjective aim of divinity, the divine lure in each moment toward truth, beauty, and goodness. This telos is also what Wilber points to in his systematic description of holons, of the vision of each piece of the universe linked to every other piece in a vast, dynamic web. And the telos of evolution toward a unified experience of divine love was the clear culmination of Teilhard's theology. This telos of evolution is a subtle but powerful force that must be felt, sensed, and intuited through the wisdom of the body, mind, and spirit working in unison.

In my pregnant state, my awareness of the telos of evolution was heightened. The sense of spiritual peace I felt stemmed from the profoundly personal and yet communal nature of the miracle unfolding inside me. This seemingly paradoxical, ambiguous experience exemplifies bodily based wisdom. Our bodies both contain and isolate us, while at the same time their needs, cycles, and history link us into a continuum of cooperation with the rest of the planetary community. The contradictions that my body embraces—its depths, its emotions, and, ultimately, its spiritual core—are those that science wants to ignore. It is in these contradictions that Osmose ultimately finds its power.

DESCARTES REVISITED

Char Davies thrives on ambiguity. As a computer artist and one of the earliest members of Softimage, a wildly successful computer animation company, Davies has become accustomed to the varied demands of the working artist and the businesswoman. As I sit in her corporate office looking through a bookshelf that mingles writings on philosophy, ecology, art, and theology with computer software theory, I am struck that this women has learned to find creative sustenance in fluidly shifting between seemingly contradictory roles. In essence, what Davies's life experience has taught her is that the journey, not the destination, is the key to creative wholeness. This insight is a perfect foil for cyberspace, a medium whose very soul is composed of movement and process.

Davies began her professional career as a painter and visual artist. She pursued these media for fifteen years, using them to explore the primary thematic material that she characterizes as the relationship between the inner, spiritual and subjective world and the outer, physical world, or what she calls nature. Davies traces her fascination with the archetypal dynamic between inner and outer to a mystical experience she had some twenty years ago. She describes herself in a field at dusk when "suddenly, for an instant the boundaries of my mind expanded to merge with the horizon, creating a sense of union between self and world that I have longed for ever since."[4] This moment in the field drove Davies to find an artistic medium capable of communicating the sensual, full-body experience that was the core of her experience.

In the mid-1980s, Davies discovered the 3-D computer animation of artist Daniel Langlois. Fasincated by the potential of his images, she sought him out. A few years later, when Langlois founded Softimage, Davies joined him and the two worked for several years to build a company dedicated to producing high-quality computer animation software. The company was enormously successful. Softimage software is widely considered the best in the computer animation industry and is responsible for the effects in such movies as *The Mask, Jurassic Park,* and *Jumanji.* In 1994, Microsoft bought Softimage. Davies left the company at the end of 1997 to pursue her artistic research separately. In her

---

4. Char Davies, "Osmose," page 5.

last three years at Softimage, she concentrated on pushing the boundaries of virtual reality as an art form. Osmose is the result of these efforts.

Davies describes Osmose as "about *being-in-the-world* in its most
profound sense, i.e., our subjective experience as sentient, embodied,
incarnate beings embedded in enveloping flowing space."[5] As an artwork, Osmose is "motivated by the desire to heal the Cartesian split
between mind/body, subject/object, which has shaped our cultural
values and contributed to our dominating stance toward (and estrange-
ment from) life. In this context, Osmose seeks to resensitize—recon-
necting mind, body and world."[6]

Davies's statement seems, at first glance, something of an oxy-
moron. Computers serving to reconnect mind, body, and world?
Davies's medium, virtual reality, has its roots in military applications. It
was originally created by the Department of Defense for flight training
simulations. Since the technology has entered the public domain, the
vast majority of implementations have continued with this theme of
simulating the real world by seeking to re-create some semblance of it,
albeit in a heightened way. VR designers constrain the medium through
"solid" walls and familiar and clearly defined "rooms" or "buildings."
Participants in VR commonly navigate these pseudo-Cartesian worlds
as though they are driving, using conventions such as pointing or joy-
sticks. This means of moving through the space emphasizes the experience of an external, objective world.

The desire to re-create our reality in a realistic and yet oddly sani-
tized form, the Holy Grail of the vast majority of VR research since its
early days, reflects many of the basic impulses in the computer graphics world in general. In 1989, the early days of VR, artist and educator

---

5. Ibid., page 3.
6. Ibid.

Richard Wright summarized this mindset when he wrote, "The perception of computer imagery . . . is one of faultless presentation, accuracy, and a commitment to the myth of self-justifying technological progress. . . . What [is sought] is a kind of 'realism' that tries to describe the world with an insistent, even authoritarian, accuracy that is overwhelming. It is as though the corporate power of the media had joined up with the methodological rigor of the mathematicians and scientists to create some final, definitive and coercive depiction of the visual world."[7]

Understood in this context, it is no surprise that we have generated a cultural confusion around cyberspace, assuming that we have to choose between organic and cyber realities. When cyberspace is held up as a better, cleaner version of organic space, we are seduced. But this seduction hides a thorny nest of problems, not the least of which is that we cannot really leave organic space behind. We are embodied creatures, and our physical, emotional, and spiritual health depends on being in our bodies in a deep and respectful manner. When we try to escape this reality, entering the computer-generated fantasies of TV and advertising, we disempower our bodily based imaginations. After all, in these hyperreal worlds, whose fantasy are we entering, and what vision drove their creation?

The heightening and objectifying of reality that still characterizes most of the implementations of cyberspace is certainly not a new desire in our culture. Robert Romanyshyn argues that one important thread in the development of a technology that encourages us to objectify the world and leave our bodies behind can be traced to the development of linear-perspective vision. This way of seeing the world emerged from a

---

7. Richard Wright, "The Image in Art and 'Computer Art,' " *Leonardo*, Computer Art Supplemental Issue, 1989, page 51.

technique developed in the 1400s in which painters literally created mathematical, life-size grids that they would place between themselves and their subjects. This practice created a firm separation between the viewer and the viewed, between self and world. In this process, the self was transformed into a spectator and the world became a spectacle. As Romanyshyn writes, "The shift is from the created order of nature to the creation of meaning established by the self in its withdrawal from the world."[8]

The self behind the window is a self that has disengaged from the physical world and from its own body to become a being of almost pure mind. We can hear in this development a clear echo of Plato's wish to move away from the messy reality of embodied experience toward the pure world of ideal forms. The outcome of this perspective is that the world through the window becomes a mathematically defined, geometric, and ultimately fragmented universe. The world that the self engages mutates into a universe of rational intellect. As Romanyshyn explains, "The hegemony of the head leaves no room for the pantomimic body, for the body with its power to generate spaces, to create situations. Within the linear, and homogeneous, space of explanation, within that grid where all space has become equal and the same, the heterogeneous pantomimic body has no place."[9] In other words, there is no room for embodied wisdom in the world of linear-perspective vision.

In their current implementation, computers seem to be propelling us further toward this disembodied place, becoming, to borrow Walker Percy's phrase, "cosmonauts in cyberspace."[10] This notion borrows from both a hope and a fear. We have the desire to escape the messy

---

8. Robert Romanyshyn, *Technology as Symptom and Dream*, page 80.

9. Ibid., page 115.

10. Walker Percy, *Lost in the Cosmos*.

and mortal sphere of the body while, at the same time, we are afraid that the alternate realities offered by cyberspace will simply suck us in, pulling us step by step away from the organic world that gave us birth. What we really want is to have our cake and eat it too. We would like to have bodies that are forever young, beautiful, and free of pain that inhabit a clean and orderly natural world free of forces beyond our control.

Walker Percy writes, "Every advance in our objective understanding of the Cosmos and its technological control further distances the self from the Cosmos precisely in the degree of the advance—so that in the end the self becomes a spacebound ghost which roams the very Cosmos it understands perfectly."[11] It may be no coincidence that cyberspace has emerged as a cultural force at this point in time. In its current form, cyberspace offers us a way to push the limits of ghosthood. Through it, we can roam the universe of information at will, our minds cast loose in the infinite, discursive Net. But in this wandering we are becoming hungry ghosts. While we cram ourselves with information, we thirst for connection, depth, and spiritual meaning in our lives. We are discovering a need for the wisdom that only our bodies and a deep experience of the natural world can bring.

There is a flip side to this story. The ghostly realm of cyberspace has the potential to push us back into the organic world with new eyes. Many astronauts who have circled the globe report awakening to a profound love for the beauty and fragility of our planet when they viewed it from afar. A similar dynamic may be in play between us and cyberspace. The particular form of understanding that can emerge in the interaction between the human and cyber worlds is precisely the point for Davies.

---

11. Ibid., pages 12–13.

When Davies immerses us in a world that explodes Cartesian space, that relies on our inner, subjective experience for its power, she seeks to "enable us to experience our place in the world afresh."[12] This is one of her primary goals, and she is fond of quoting Gaston Bachelard to emphasize the point: ". . . by changing space, by leaving the space of one's usual sensibilities, one enters into communication with a space that is psychically innovating. . . . For we do not change place, we change our Nature."[13] The ambiguous, fluid, and spatially unfamiliar world of Osmose—where the virtual body hovers and floats in a digital terrain unhampered by gravity—opens our senses for a new relationship to the organic world when we reenter it. It is Davies's hope that these various elements in Osmose will "work together to loosen the mind's rational hold, dissolving the subject/object dichotomy, and, in a dream-like way, [shift] the immersant's mode of experience away from the everyday bias of eyesight to one that resonates deeper within the physical body."[14]

In eliciting a paradoxical experience of embodiment, Osmose invites us to reexamine the relationship between bodies and cyberspace. Osmose is an abstract space that calls us to be *grounded* in our physical bodies. In it we are embodied and disembodied simultaneously. As Davies writes, "In Osmose, this paradox is amplified. After a certain period of immersion (usually about ten minutes), various conditions related to the imagery, luminosity, semitransparency, spatial ambiguity, slow subtle transitions between the worlds, evocative resonant sounds, along with solitude, deep breathing and maintaining one's center of balance within the space all combine to create a distinct shift of awareness

---

12. Char Davies, "Osmose," page 1.
13. Ibid.
14. Ibid., page 3.

as he or she lets go of the rational urge to control, and boundaries between inner, outer, mind, body, space and time begin to dissolve."[15]

Paradox has a special role to play on the road to spiritual awareness. Perhaps the most fundamental paradox in our experience is that between mind and body. Spiritual experience can reconcile this paradox as it enables us to feel a connection to all that is from the locus of bodies that clearly keep us separate. We are connected and yet disconnected at the same time. The enabling force in this reconciliation is "transcendence," or what many traditions refer to as "nonduality." As Ken Wilber explains, "Paradox is simply the way nonduality looks to the mental level. Spirit itself is not paradoxical; it is not characterizable at all."[16]

Accessing the transcendent aspect of spirit enables us to move beyond the paradoxes generated by the mind and its relationship to body and spirit into a place of oneness. From the transcendent perspective, paradox dissolves. As Wilber reminds us, paradox is a condition generated by mind. Therefore, paradox and ambiguity can serve as signals that we are in the realm of mind. Reconciliation and wholeness require incorporation of an experience of spirit. As an integrative space that brings together the cyber and the bodily, the worlds of code and text with the dreamscapes of artistic vision, Osmose comprises a hopeful next step as we struggle to integrate the complex and confusing contradictions represented by cyber, spirit, and body.

---

15. Ibid., page 6.

16. Ken Wilber, *Eye to Eye*, page 180.

EMBODIED WISDOM

The language of the body speaks in a mysterious tongue for those of us born and raised in Western, scientific culture. Embodied wisdom is not revealed by our outer gaze. We cannot see it, dissect it, or objectify it. This wisdom arises through the worlds of sensation and emotion, realms we have been enculturated to ignore. Fueled by intuitive imagination and galvanized by a deeply felt experience of bodily reality, this wisdom covers a spectrum of sensation, from excruciating pain to sublime pleasure, from transcendent moments of sexual bliss to the terrifying knowledge of our mortality. In all of its guises, bodily wisdom can be one of our greatest teachers.

Bodily wisdom transforms the body from a collection of atoms to an awesome process that is more than the sum of its parts. The deeper wisdom of the body is accessed through an understanding of the larger processes that guide the universe, of the primal truth that life is a journey, a continual unfolding and becoming. Embodied wisdom, which speaks in circles, not lines, is a direct link into the sacred, connecting us not only to the earth but also to the possibility of a creative divinity that reaches beyond the mind into the soul and spirit of each of us.

All world religions have long histories of embodied practice that serve to join the whole of who we are with an experience of divinity. In the Hindu tradition, Hatha Yoga, one of the eight limbs of yogic practice, offers a profound, bodily based meditative practice. In Islam, the tradition of Sufi dancing brings the practitioner closer to his or her God. Fasting, vision quests, ritual feasts, and breath work—some variety of these practices can be found in most religious traditions. As theologian Margaret Miles has amply demonstrated in her book *The Fullness of Life,* we in the West have a long and profound tradition of embodied practice, a tradition that we would be wise to recall as we reach into a future saturated with the potentially disembodied networks of cyberspace.

The Western tradition of embodied spiritual practice is most often referred to as "asceticism." Contrary to popular belief, argues Miles, ascetic practices are not intended to deny or harm the body. When undertaken correctly, these practices enable us to achieve greater self-understanding, overcome habituation and addiction, gather and focus energy, change our cultural conditioning, and intensify or expand our consciousness. Rediscovering these practices offers a means for us to honor the tradition of our past while simultaneously reaching forward toward increased vitality, human dignity, and freedom.

Asceticism as Miles presents it is essentially a series of disciplined, life-enhancing practices that enable one to achieve a greater unity of soul and body. She is careful to distinguish between positive forms of asceticism and those forms that were based on the "idea of a closed energy system in which the soul gathers energy at the expense of the body."[17] These beliefs she refers to as the "old asceticism," which she claims to be punitive and masochistic, depending on an antagonistic attitude between mind and body. This old asceticism, she points out, remains with us in another form today. Many of us are deeply addicted to behaviors that steal from the body to soothe the psyche—habits such as drug and alcohol dependency, overeating, and overwork. These practices damage our bodies, deaden our connection to our souls, and inhibit the natural unity of our beings. As Miles argues, the reclaiming of healthy ascetic practices can help us to overcome these addictive behaviors.

Asceticism in the West can be traced back to the early Christian era (the fourth and fifth centuries), when scores of men and women fled the

---

17. Margaret Miles, *The Fullness of Life,* page 156.

cities to undertake lives of spiritual rigor in the Egyptian desert. These early adepts, as the ascetic Palladius wrote, "wished to lay hold upon their souls."[18] In order to do this, they needed to quiet the turmoil that characterized both their inner and outer worlds. It was only then that they could hear the still, small voice of the divine.

Quieting the turmoil of the outer world began, for the most part, by living lives of solitude. But solitude was only a first step. Many ascetics found that in their solitude, the turmoil of their inner lives grew more powerful. In order to achieve the much more difficult goal of inner peace, the ascetics strove for a high degree of self-knowledge. It was only through intimate knowledge of one's "demons" and "passions" that one could move beyond the anxieties and inner conflicts that kept one from, as Evagrius wrote, "a habitual state of imperturbable calm" wherein the soul is "snatched to the heights of intelligible reality . . . by the most intense love."[19]

In the quest for self-knowledge and deep and lasting spiritual experience, the body had a central role to play. As Miles explains, ascetic practices assumed that "the discipline learned by the body is also gained by the soul."[20] In the same vein, the ascetics were wary of abusing the body, as such abuse would also wreak havoc on the soul. Ascetic masters taught a careful regime of practices used in the right measure at the correct time. Bodily based practices included reading, vigils, prayer, fasting, solitude, continence, and limiting water intake. Continence for these early practitioners meant controlling bodily passions such as gluttony and lust through "refusing with joy."

While some of this might sound vaguely alarming to us today, the

---

18. Ibid., page 136.
19. Ibid., page 40.
20. Ibid., page 139.

underlying process of achieving greater self-knowledge through practices that integrate body, mind, and spirit remain central to our attempts to create lives of spiritual wisdom and clarity. As Miles writes, "The claim made by the Egyptian desert ascetics was that bodily practices intimately affect the psyche and can be used as a method for exploring one's characteristically well-defended psychic agenda, for understanding those unconscious but powerful insecurities, anxieties, and angers which strip the psyche of energy and undermine its conscious attempts at joyous and loving being."[21]

These techniques must be understood in the context of their times. Certain practices, such as lifelong celibacy, seem repugnant to us today. Others, such as the "penances" that became popular in the monastic era, hint of masochism. But as Miles points out, this was a pre-Freudian world, a world where extreme measures were often necessary to submerge one in the self-knowledge that is such a crucial step in the journey toward living a life based in spirit. In spite of our differences with the particulars of these models, there are some basic truths that can be gleaned from them. These truths form the basis of "positive asceticism."

Positive asceticism is founded on a series of primary insights. The first is that the body and the soul are intimate partners. When the body is altered by ascetic practice, the soul is altered as well. If the body remains in a pattern of habitual behavior with regard to its interaction with the world, if it engages with drugs, sex, or food habitually and unconsciously, the soul too will remain in habitual and unconscious patterns. It follows that ascetic practices should be "fully as good for body as for soul."[22] Positive asceticism resolutely does not include wearing hair shirts, endless fasting, or self-flagellation.

---

21. Ibid., page 141.
22. Ibid., page 160.

Ascetic practices should be undertaken only on a temporary basis and should be directed clearly and specifically toward a particular problem. With this end in mind, Miles points to a set of ascetic practices that she calls "perennially useful." These include short fasts, meditation, prayer, and breathing exercises. In our information-saturated world, Miles recommends fasting not only from food and alcohol but also from the media for a period of time, allowing ourselves time to experience the world in a new way.

Positive asceticism reminds us that disciplined, bodily based practices help us to wake up and make conscious choices. Conscious choice-making has profound implications not only for our personal and spiritual lives but also for the communal life we live on this planet. When spiritual practice is grounded in such simple activities as eating, sleeping, and walking along the city streets, each aspect of one's life has the potential of being consciously chosen. Practices such as these naturally raise our self-awareness, enabling us to access portions of our psyches that are usually clouded from view.

What all ascetic practices point to is the unavoidable truth that what we *do* is as important as what we *think*. Changing what we do, not just what we think, is what really counts in the end. As Miles writes, "If we take seriously the admonition that changes in the habits and condition of the body open the soul to greater insight, we understand the need for a new asceticism. We find ourselves cluttered with habits and addictions that deaden our sense of lifefulness."[23] Disciplined practice grounds choice in the body, enlivening and strengthening both body and spirit. In this context, faith in the power of spirit to transform one's life becomes a lived reality.

We now stand at a new stage, one in which we struggle to move

---

23. Ibid., page 163.

to the next step in the evolution of our embodied wisdom and practice. This new wisdom must blend the discoveries of science with the
world of feeling and intuition. We cannot go back to the ways of our
ancestors; their world was fundamentally different from ours. We
are not intimately involved in making or producing our food, cloth-
ing, and shelter. Our bodily needs are no longer the center of gravity of our experience. What we can glean from the past, however, is
insight into a type of wisdom that we crave, a wisdom based on an
experience of spirit infusing all of who we are. How we achieve this
goal in a world that seems increasingly inimical to our bodies is a
challenge that each of us must meet in his or her own way. One
thing is clear, however: This challenge will require that we activate
our rational, spiritual, and embodied imaginations in a fundamentally new way. In this quest, cyberspace may have a particular role
to play.

BODiES iN CYBERSPACE

The two-dimensional, data-centric interfaces that we currently employ
to enter cyberspace offer only the merest glimmer of the true nature and
potential of the medium. In the point-and-click interface, data objects
in the form of menus, icons, and soft buttons objectify our interaction
with the world of cyberspace. It should come as no surprise, in this context, that we tend to think the world of cyberspace is made up solely of
two-dimensional objects. Like the technique of perspective vision, the
window through which we view the world models the world that we
see. Two-dimensional interfaces mask from view the fundamental,
process-oriented nature of the digital world.

The creation of deep participation in cyberspace has proved an elusive goal. While sacred experiences can be had within the context of the two-dimensional, text, and symbol-based interfaces of today, they are more of an unexpected accident than an intentional activity. But according to Brenda Laurel, a VR pioneer and media theorist, and to Char Davies, virtual reality offers a promising alternative. Laurel writes that VR "was not a logical successor to the brain-in-a-box. In fact, VR turned computers inside out. The brain-in-a-box computer has no body; VR uses our bodies as its instrument. Rather than presenting framed pictures or pull-down menus, VR gives us a first-person, body-centric view. Computers—even today's frisky little portables—immobilize the body in front of a keyboard and screen; conversely, VR relies upon human movement and kinesthetic sensations to achieve its effect. VR qualifies as what Marshall McLuhan described as an 'anti-environment'—an inversion that turns the existing environment into an object of attention, scrutiny, and criticism."[24]

The environments in which we find ourselves, the places in which our bodies reside, situate us in a particular point of view. As I sit in front of my PowerBook writing these words, my intellect is functioning at the forefront of my experience. When I take a break, rise from my desk, and walk to the window to observe the overcast sky and a group of people talking in the street below, my mind relaxes. The inner and the outer worlds connect; the experiences of the body affect the mind and the soul. Entering a world in which archetypal elements form the primary experience of reality invites us to transcend our enculturated sense of objective embodiment. This experience is clearly at the heart of the power of Osmose. It is also the goal of Placeholder, a virtual reality

---

24. Brenda Laurel, "The Ethos of Computing," prepared for ACM 97, available at: http://www.tauzero.com/Brenda_Laurel/Severed_Heads

environment created by Brenda Laurel, Rachel Strickland, and Rob Tow of Interval Research Corporation.

Placeholder, an immersive, interactive research project undertaken at the Banff Centre in Alberta, Canada, explores the relationship between place and narrative in the context of a virtual performance piece. Placeholder simultaneously immersed two participants in a series of three virtual environments whose images were drawn from video footage of three actual locations in Banff National Park—a hot spring located inside a cave, a waterfall in a canyon, and a series of rock formations perched above a river. Rachel Strickland explains that the goal of using this quasi-documentary technique was to capture the *genus loci,* or the "guardian spirit of the place." This was achieved in part through identifying and enhancing the particular qualities of each place. "For example," Strickland writes, "it was determined that the waterfall model should incorporate video to render the dynamic flow of the water. The sense of the cave should be auditory rather than visual—a dimly illuminated quick sketch surrounding a lively array of localized sound sources."[25]

The narrative elements that led people through the virtual landscapes were drawn from Neolithic and Paleolithic myth and iconography. The designers of the piece elected to create four "spirit critters"—spider, snake, fish, and crow—that the participants would embody through the use of "smart costumes." Once a participant took on the body of the critter, he or she would move, speak, and even see from the critter's perspective. This convention had the effect of highlighting the experience of being embodied in new and different ways. Laurel reports that once most people embodied a critter, they began to

---

25. Brenda Laurel et al., "Placeholder," available at:
   http://www.tauzero.com/Brenda__Laurel/Severed__Heads

act and move as that critter would, further opening the possibilities for narrative play in the environment. Laurel comments, "If VR is to be used as a medium for narrative, dramatic, or playful activity, we should question the appropriateness of conventions derived from computer displays, teleoperations or training simulators. . . . Our motto was 'no interface,' expressing our desire to maximize naturalness, to enable the body to act directly in the world, and to minimize distraction and cognitive load."[26]

Participants moved among the three locations through a series of active portals marked by the image of a spiral. As participants approached a portal, they heard ambient noises generated by another of the spaces. When they entered the portal, they experienced ten seconds of darkness, while still hearing the sounds from the space they would emerge into. When they arrived at the space, the active area was defined by a "magic circle" approximately ten feet in diameter. While both the portals and the magic circles were to some extent restricted by the technical limitations of the medium (the size of the magic circles was determined by the range of the VR equipment), they offered participants an experience of journeying through the environments, guided in a loose way by ancient and psychically resonant images.

As Placeholder and Osmose demonstrate in nascent form, the hidden power of virtual reality lies in its ability to help us feel ourselves in new ways. As Laurel writes about Placeholder, "Working on this piece has demonstrated to me that the art of designing in VR is really the art of creating spaces with qualities that call forth active imagination. The VR artist does not bathe the participant in content; she invites the participant to produce content by constructing meanings, to experience the pleasure of embodied imagination."[27]

---

26. Ibid.
27. Ibid.

Virtual reality represents only one strategy in the quest for engaging an embodied experience in cyberspace. Its technological conventions—the head set, data gloves, and motion-tracking sensors—will soon be usurped by more sophisticated technical solutions. But whatever direction technology takes, VR as implemented by Davies and Laurel offers us an important example. By giving us a different way in, it shows us that how we approach cyberspace matters. If we look at cyberspace through a window, we will see a world much like the early perspective painters saw through their mathematical grids—a world of objective, divided, geometric forms. If, however, we enter it through a doorway that enables us to bring all of our senses along, an entirely new experience emerges.

PAYiNG ATTEnTiOn

Our bodies, with their particular points of view, imaginative abilities, and environmental surroundings, are where the divine spirit is revealed to us. Theologian Sally McFague suggests a powerful model for imaging this fundamental truth. McFague invites us to conceive of the universe as God's body. In this model, God is related to the universe as our own unique spirit is to our bodies. For McFague, spirit is the "breath of life," a notion that clearly echoes John Cobb's vision of God as Life. As McFague writes, "Each of us . . . owes our existence, breath by breath as we inhale and exhale, to God. We 'live and move and have our being' in God (Acts 17:28). Indeed we do. That is, perhaps, the most basic confession that can be made: I owe my existence at its most fundamental level—the gift of my next breath—to God. God is my creator and recreator, the One who gives and renews my life, moment by moment, at its most basic, physical level. And so does everything else in creation (also life), moment by moment, by the breath of God."[28]

McFague argues that God's transcendent nature makes itself felt in the world in a way that is both concrete and awesome. It is only through our embodied selves that we can experience some glimmer of divine transcendence. When we move into the realms of wonder, awe, and magnificence, that is when the divine reveals itself to us. Revelation is the visceral experience of being connected to a larger, spirit-infused reality where the borders between self and other blur. In this context, the universe, God's body, "serves as a deep reflecting pool of divine magnificence and grandeur. To contemplate what we know of the universe, from the extraordinary ordinariness of a butterfly's wing to the ordinary extraordinariness of the Milky Way, is beyond all our capacities of imagination: the longer we reflect on either of these phenomena, the more filled with wonder we become."[29]

As McFague reminds us, it is not just the experience of the oneness of creation that causes us to marvel, but the realization that this oneness is composed of an infinite diversity of embodied forms. In this sense, the creation story that the sciences tell us may be one of the most potent meditations on divinity we can contemplate. When we come to understand the incredible age, size, breadth, depth, and complexity of the natural world coupled with the phenomenal ways in which human culture has woven itself through history, we stand in hushed awe before the divine, creative power that helped to render such a fantastic array.

For McFague, meditating on the differences in the universe is one of the primary sacraments for engaging the sacred nature of God's

---

28. Sally McFague, *The Body of God,* page 144.

29. Ibid., page 154.

body. She calls this "attention epistemology"[30] and claims it as a central feature of sacred embodied wisdom. Embodied wisdom requires honoring our distinct and particular points of view without resorting to divisive individualism. Attention epistemology offers a way of claiming the distinctive embodiment of all aspects of creation while cleaving to the reality that we are all woven together with divine spirit. This is ultimately the lesson of positive asceticism—self-knowledge leads to a deep understanding that each self has its own, unique perspective to contribute to the larger whole of creation. As Yahweh saw at the beginning of the universe, there were differences and they were good.

Attention to difference can both teach and transform. It teaches us that through paying close attention to the uniqueness of all of creation, through respecting and honoring diversity, we can find spiritual connection. Through attention, we engage both our differences and our connections. This experience can transform us into moral beings who act with care and respect for our bodies and the world in all its divine diversity.

Cyberspace represents an utterly different, new, and unknown world for us. As we begin to learn how to engage it in richer and more multivalent ways, we will return to organic reality transformed. We will have new subjectivities, new experiences to incorporate. We will no longer be who we were. Our best hope for creating transformations that are spiritually evolutionary in nature will entail engaging an embodied wisdom that begins by paying attention at the deepest level to the whole of creation.

---

30. Ibid., page 49 and following.

(8)

VIRTUAL ETHICS

In February 1997, I received the following e-mail, forwarded from a friend to a list of dozens of friends and colleagues.

>>>Dear friends:

>>>Tonight at 11:30 PM (local time) several thousand policemen attacked the Belgrade demonstrators. I've just come back from the town, and as a witness I can say this:

>>>We were blocked in front of the Branko's bridge for more than 2 hours. 10-15,000 people were on the other side of the bridge, but police blocked the bridge from both sides, and did not allow them to join us. There were 30-40,000 people on our side of the bridge, but many of them left the place. When only 4-5,000 remained, and when we saw that

strong police forces began to circle us, the opposition leader Vuk Draskovic spoke, and told us to
go to the center—because 5-10 minutes before that
we felt that perhaps they would attack. We started
to go, and less than a minute later police attacked
us from all sides with water cannons and tear gas.
There was NO provocation from our side, and there
was NO one single reason for the police to attack!
We began to retreat and run away, but the police
started running after the people, beating brutally
everyone whom they could catch—older women, children, everyone without difference. A taxi driver
took me and my wife and drove us home. Now I am
listening to the two independent radio stations
here (B92 and Radio Index): several thousand
policemen are on the streets in the center of Belgrade beating everyone there! People try to escape,
but at the moment the situation is dangerous around
the Faculty of philosophy where many people found
a shelter. The latest news is that policemen
entered into the Faculty, beat several people and
arrested many others. Hundred of people are
injured. Many cameramen were attacked. In a dramatic interview Vuk Draskovic just said that police
fired at him, but somehow he managed to escape—he
says that the regime gave orders to kill him this
night. The lady from the opposition, the leader of
pacifist Civil Ligue of Serbia Vesna Pesic is
injured. At the time I am writing this message, the
police action still goes on!

>>>Please, help us by informing everyone on the net about this terrible night in Belgrade.

>>>And we are going to keep fighting for our freedom and rights, no doubt! They can arrest us, but they cannot win, no matter what happens!

>>>Yours, Novica Milic

I proceeded to disseminate this message to my list. I can only assume that the people I sent it to forwarded it as well. Critical, politically sensitive information travels the Net in this fashion every day. There are hundreds, if not thousands, of examples of e-mail and the WWW enabling political change and grassroots activism. Human rights abuses are routinely communicated, and vast resources on global pollution and environmental abuses are readily available. On-line databases stuffed with sensitive social and environmental information serve as clearinghouses for countless political actions, community-based groups, and global communities of interest. Portable computers linked into the global satellite network enable people in remote locations—such as doctors, teachers, students, aid workers, and political organizers—to link quickly into a broad base of knowledge and community, often improving or saving lives as a result.

For those with access and training, computers offer unprecedented resources for political organization and social change. Those without access, however, are falling increasingly by the wayside. This imbalance is one small example of the enormous ethical and moral implications offered by computer technology. To begin to address these issues, we must look at computers in terms of their relationship to the whole of a creation whose animating and unifying force is spirit. In order for computers to realize their full sacred potential—and for us to achieve ours—it is imperative that we include them in a conscious, sacred vision of ethical behavior and moral responsibility. What we choose to *do* with our knowledge of spirit is, in the final analysis, the most important expression of our sacred lives.

THE DARK SIDE

The very first program written to run one of the earliest functional computers was used to help build the hydrogen bomb.[1] Computers have, in a very real sense, given humanity the terrifying power to wage nuclear war. Fifty years later, computers serve as the functional foundation of much warfare in general, as evidenced most recently by the Gulf War, a conflict that the media dubbed the "first virtual war." A recent report by the Rand Corporation[2] focuses on the phenomenon of what they call "strategic information warfare" (IW), or the role of potentially vulnerable computer systems in future global conflicts. In this vision, computers will not only help engineer, build, and deploy weapons, but will also create a new arena for warfare to take place in. In IW, the targets are the computer systems themselves.

In IW, there is no "front line," there are no traditional boundaries, attack can be waged from any geography with relatively inexpensive equipment, and traditional intelligence methods fall by the wayside. The enemy in IW can be a small, nimble gang of hackers, terrorists, or

---

1. John Young, "Global Network," page 47.

2. Roger Molander, Andrew Riddile, Peter Wilson, *Strategic Information Warfare: A New Face of War,* Rand Corporation, 1996, abstract available at: http://www.rand.com

disaffected citizens working with meager and highly mobile resources. Not only could the enemy be difficult to locate in an information war, but the very fact of the war itself may be hard to spot. Random power outages, disrupted transportation systems—technical glitch or strategic attack? In the brave new world of IW, the line between the military and the citizenry is blurred. Casualties in both camps could come from attacks on computer systems that result in catastrophic disruptions to transportation, energy, supplies of food and water, and the distribution of medical supplies. Since these systems are global in nature, an IW waged on any major developed country could have immediate and devastating global implications.

Computer networks present major vulnerabilities in peacetime as well. The impact that computers have on our privacy, on our ability to communicate openly and freely, and on our control over the fruits of our intellectual lives are serious areas of contention very much in the process of working themselves out. The fights between the powers that want to monitor and limit our information consumption and dissemination and those who claim that information should be free are among the most important social debates of our time. The outcome of issues such as copyright protection, "eavesdropping" devices such as the Clipper chip, and the Communications Decency Act (CDA) will have deep and long-lasting ethical and moral implications. No one can afford to remain uninformed or uninvolved when it comes to these policy battles.

Class divisions, social justice, and economic disadvantage comprise another realm in which computers are currently exerting a profoundly debilitating moral impact. The divide between the so-called information haves and the have-nots is growing dramatically. This divide has a disproportionately large effect on the urban poor. In the last thirty years, residents of the center cities of the United States have become increasingly poor and unemployed. The causes of this decline are complex, having to do with decreases in public support and charitable funds, the migration of jobs out of the center cities, and a drop in public housing, among other factors. The end result is that on average, 22 percent of inner-city residents fall below the poverty line. These figures are even higher for children. While poverty levels for whites and African-Americans have declined, Hispanic poverty levels have increased to fill the gap. In neighborhoods with high concentrations of extreme poverty, social pathology such as "personal and property crime, drug dependency, family breakdown, children born to teenagers, infant death rate, low birth weight, child abuse and stress related diseases" are growing.[3]

Computers are not directly responsible for this grim picture, but they are exacerbating an already bad situation. In well-funded suburbia, children are busily preparing to join the information economy. On-line computer usage among young people is overwhelmingly concentrated in affluent suburban areas where the public schools are routinely stocked with functional and current technology. In low-income areas, the primary contact between teenagers and computers comes in the form of shoot-'em-up arcade games. For families whose major worries are the daily safety of their children and making ends meet, a computer seems a distant reality at best. In addition, many of the public assistance programs aimed at training inner-city youth to use computers have been cut back.

This situation is further compounded by the fact that jobs in the computer industry are located far from the inner cities, centered primarily in affluent suburban areas. As increasing amounts of power and wealth are channeled to those who run the computer industry, the

---

3. Analysis and quote from Julian Wolpert, "Session Summary from Center Cities as Havens and Traps for Low-Income Communities," page 4, available at: http://sap.mit.edu/projects/colloquium/

demographics of diversity in that industry remain abysmal. The computer elite is primarily white and male. Minorities, when they are present, are concentrated in low-level positions. According to industry observer John Young, "Only 17% of the semi-skilled production workers are white males, while 63% are women—of whom half are nonwhite."[4] There is little or no attempt by technology companies to train disadvantaged or minority people for the few entry-level jobs available. In fact, the investment necessary to create new information-technology jobs now exceeds, by at least four times, the cost of maintaining the average welfare household.[5] This creates a culture that, relative to many other major industries, is for the most part intolerant of minority subcultures. As Julian Wolpert, a professor of urban studies at MIT, comments, high tech is "supposed to be an industry that allows for alternative life styles. It hasn't been true. They let you dress in jeans, but there's a great deal of homogeneity among their people."[6] In the final analysis, the computer revolution seems not only to be passing the neediest by, but exacerbating their situation by draining jobs away from the center cities.

The information gap is also being felt on a global level in a variety of disturbing ways. Those who remain outside the magic loop of access and power afforded by computation don't necessarily escape exploitation by it. The phenomenon of "electronic colonialism" is being felt by underprivileged people the world over. Rejane Spitz, a Brazilian artist, argues that computers represent a powerful force of cultural domination. She writes, "Computer technology's potential to transform the

---

4. John Young, "Global Network," page 14.

5. Ibid., page 4.

6. Julian Wolpert, "Session Summary from Center Cities as Havens and Traps for Low-Income Communities," page 8.

world into a great network of communication may be its most dangerous aspect for developing nations. The egalitarian appearance of this
potential hides the fact that leadership in the development of new technologies and the design of new trends, as well as the power to spread
and control these new developments, will still be restricted to a few
hands."[7] In the current business model used by the computer industry,
the particular, highly contextualized needs of indigenous and disem-
powered peoples rates barely a nod. As a result, these people, including
those in our own inner cities, are being forced further to the margins of
the contemporary world.

Computers have negative environmental as well as social impact.
Computers have long been heralded as "clean" technology, with chips
produced in rooms so spotless that even the dust is filtered out. But as
Young points out, "The electronics industry uses a large number of
toxic or environmentally hazardous substances, many of which escape
into workspaces and the environment. While the air in 'clean rooms'
may be dustfree, it is still often contaminated with hazardous chemical
vapors."[8] Silicon Valley, a center of extraordinary wealth and rapid
growth, now harbors well over one hundred hazardous waste dump
sites, including twenty-three that have been designated as Superfund
sites by the EPA, indicating that they are among the most hazardous in
the country. Some of the most dangerous chemicals, such as trichloro-
ethylene (TCE), have leaked into the groundwater, where it is virtually
impossible to get rid of. A variety of studies suggest that higher rates of
miscarriage and birth defects may be the result of exposure to TCE.
While many of the toxic sites, located in the poorer areas of the region,

7. Rejane Spitz, "Qualitative, Dialectical and Experiential Domains of Electronic Art,"
   page 32.
8. John Young, page 37.

are slowly being cleaned up after much pressure from citizens' groups, much remains to be done. In the meantime, many U.S. companies have moved their manufacturing offshore, primarily to Asia, where environmental regulations are more lax.

In addition to these obvious ills, many critics have pointed out the more subtle, dehumanizing tendencies of computation, echoing themes that have been touched on repeatedly in this book. In pulling us away from our bodies, computers can fragment us from the whole of who we are. As fragmented beings, it becomes more difficult for us to create deep connection with one another and with the body of God, the earth itself. As we sit clicking away, isolated in front of our flickering screens, we create the potential to sacrifice a rich, embodied experience of the local for a superficial, mentalized experience of the global.

Albert Borgmann, a philosopher of technology, claims that computers mask from view the "means" that lead to the "ends" in our daily life. We no longer chop wood and carry water; we turn up the thermostat and turn on the tap. Borgmann argues that this alienates us from deep participation in the world around us, forcing us to glide from point to point along the surfaces of reality. In obscuring the means of a device while providing easy access to its ends, technology alienates us from the deeper processes of life and leads us to a shallow, ends-hungry, consumer culture.

In the face of these biting criticisms of computers stand a host of positive effects of information technology. Computers connect us, offering unprecedented means for global and local communication. In this sense, they have the potential to enable the development of genuine, global understanding. Just one computer can link a whole dissident movement to the outside world, empowering activists in repressive states in unprecedented ways. Computers are also essential to the process of cleaning up the global environment. Without the power of computing, we would be at a loss to communicate the problems of environmental degradation, to make policy decisions based on thorough understanding, or to undertake clean-up campaigns. Computers could also make local and global political action more effective, potentially revivifying the democratic process.

On a more subtle level, computers open the doorway for new, yet-undreamed-of levels of creative participation in the sacred process of evolution. But evolution guided by spirit does not always result in what we can consider "positive" outcomes. Listening to the call of spirit as it guides us toward the good, the just, and the beautiful requires constant ethical vigilance based on spiritual understanding. A positive coevolution with computers—guided from conscious, sacred knowledge—is one of humanity's greatest challenges and potentials as we enter the new millennium.

RICHNESS OF EXPERIENCE

As we undertake the daunting task of including computers in our sacred evolution, we need a broad set of ethical guidelines to steer the way. These guidelines must reflect the sacred sensibility of evolutionary process embedded in our unique, embodied awareness.

Our ethical legacy tends to be based on the idea of a clear set of moral laws that exist, like the scientific laws of nature or the Ten Commandments, objectively. It has traditionally been through these laws—such as "thou shalt not kill"—that we make ethical decisions. With the rise of the subjective self in the latter part of the twentieth century, a new breed of ethics has emerged that can best be characterized as situational. From this perspective, every ethical decision must be understood in a radically subjective context. For example, in certain circumstances, killing may be acceptable. The problem with these two extremes is that they are just that—extreme. The better path toward a functional ethical framework lies in blending the two approaches. Good ethical decisions must be understood in context and yet guided by the faith that there is a sacred unfolding in the world that exists independently of our personal experience.

Any discussion of ethics begins with an understanding of values. What is it that we value and why? What matters most? This discussion can best be broken down into two types of values—intrinsic and instrumental. Intrinsic value is the value a being has for itself, its inherent worth. Instrumental value is the value a thing has for someone or something else, the means to an end. Charles Birch and John Cobb, in their book *The Liberation of Life*, offer a framework for ethical conduct that blends these subjective and objective understandings of value.

According to the process view, the world is not composed of discrete, objective things but of events unfolding in time, fueled by divine creativity. Within this vast process, each event has some subjective experience. This experience may not be conscious, as it is for humans, but the very participation of each entity in the larger environment results in some level of experience. The ability to experience the world and participate in the force of divine creative unfolding is what gives each entity its intrinsic value.

Our inherited understanding of ethics flies in the face of this view. Most ethical systems in the West have been heavily colored by an anthropocentric, instrumental perspective. All "others," from people unlike ourselves to the lilies in the field, have been assigned value according to their usefulness to us. This instrumental vision was the root of the practice of slavery, and today it underlies such commonly accepted moral notions as dividing the organic world into an inventory of "natural resources" to be used at will. When we shift toward a sacred view of the universe as composed of a myriad of interconnecting nodes of value, the moral clarity of a solely instrumental view becomes murky at best. As a starting point for ethical reflection, the notion of the universe composed of entities with intrinsic value—from the atom to the human to the star—moves us toward a viewpoint that includes the divine.

When we experience the world as an interconnected sphere pregnant with value and potential, the opportunity to treat it differently emerges. From within this sphere, we come to see that all of creation is worthy of love and respect. With this experience as its starting point, an ethic based on the intrinsic value of all aspects of creation embraces a radically open and receptive approach to the world. Birch and Cobb characterize this ethical approach through their evocative phrase "richness of experience."

Richness of experience refers to the ability of everything that is to manifest divine creativity in the world. When, in each moment of unfolding, an entity follows the "subjective aim" of the divine, it reaches toward the life-giving forces of goodness and love, enriching not only its own experience but also that of the whole of creation. As Birch and Cobb remind us, "life *is* experience. To have richer experience is to be more alive."[9] To be more alive is synonymous with being increasingly filled with divine spirit. Thus, richness of experience refers to an ethic of manifesting divine creativity and love wherever possible.

As self-conscious beings, we have a particular and somewhat confusing role to play in the pursuit of richness of experience. Our con-

---

9. Charles Birch and John Cobb, *The Liberation of Life*, page 146.

scious intellect is a mixed blessing. Because of it, we appear to be the "crown of creation." Our brain power makes us enormously influential, enabling us to feel that we are the center of the universe. But in an interconnected universe, the attribute of self-consciousness is only one contribution among the multitude of richness contributed by the plants, animals, stars, wind, and rain. The intrinsic value of the whole universe far exceeds that of any one of us. The whole is greatly enriched by the participation of the multitudes. Knowing this, we must devise ways of acting from the knowledge that we are simultaneously equal and yet unequal to the rest of creation. We are a part of the stream of evolution and yet in some very real ways we are guiding it forward. In other words, we must develop a nonanthropocentric ethic from an inescapably anthropocentric perspective.

An ethic based on the goal of richness of experience begins with a general principle: Act in ways that maximize value in general both for humans and for the nonhuman world. Value in this case refers both to an entity's intrinsic worth or richness of experience *and* its instrumental benefit or value for others. The best ethical decisions are based on pursuing both of these values, balancing the enhancement of richness of experience with a realistic assessment of the instrumental value involved. As Birch and Cobb point out, living ethically is not a science, but the art of learning to blend facts with faith, grace, and empathy.

In order to achieve this difficult feat, it is helpful if a scale of relative value is devised. Everything we do affects in a potentially compromising way everything else, be it an atom, a plant, or another human. If all things have equal intrinsic value and each entity's intrinsic value is infinite, ethical action would become impossible. But the intrinsic value of an atom is not the same as that of a human. In fact, the ability of an atom to realize richness of experience is so relatively small as to be, for practical purposes, almost insignificant. An atom therefore can be thought of primarily from the perspective of its instrumental value as a building block of creation. Based on judgments of this sort, Cobb and Birch erect a rough hierarchy of value ranging from atoms to cells, plants, animals, and humans.

On the lower rungs of the ladder—composed first of atoms, then cells, then plants—the values are primarily, though not wholly, instrumental. When we reach the level of animals, the balance begins to tip. With the introduction of complex nervous systems, conscious feeling is born. Consciousness greatly increases the potential richness of experience of a being, and thus its intrinsic value rises. In the case of animals, "their existence and enjoyment is important, regardless of the consequences for us or other entities . . . In short, they make a claim upon us, and we have duties toward them."[10] We have an ethical duty to avoid actions that prevent richness of experience in the animal kingdom. This includes a strong duty to protect against the extinction of any species. This leads to an ethic of reasoned compromise between the human and animal worlds, particularly those animals with more complex nervous systems. In Birch and Cobb's view, inflicting suffering and loss on animals is ethically acceptable only if the human instrumental gain is truly enormous in comparison.

The domain of humans in this hierarchy of rights forms its own distinct category. The traditional religious view has been that humans have infinite intrinsic value and therefore human life must be protected at all costs. But no human being has an infinite capacity for richness of experience, and therefore Birch and Cobb disagree with those who argue for the protection of human life in all circumstances. They argue that when human life reaches a point where the ability to experience richness decreases dramatically, such as when a person falls into a long-term

---

10. Ibid., page 153.

coma, it is ethically acceptable to end that life. The issue for human rights is not blind protection of life regardless of circumstance, but an ethical injunction to create environments that enhance and extend the creative abilities of all human beings.

Self-conscious understanding is the hallmark of human life. We can make conscious choices to accept or reject the creative force of divine life, of rich experience. In this sense, we are all equal. We may not have infinite intrinsic value, but we have *equal* intrinsic value in relation to one another. Although some people may have greater instrumental value than others, everyone's intrinsic value is the same. This equality in our capacity for richness of experience forms the center of the ethic of human rights and responsibilities.

It is clear from looking around that even though we all have equal potential for rich experience, our achievement of it varies widely. There are many reasons for this, ranging from economic and cultural inequalities to disparate childhood experiences. Inequality, as Birch and Cobb point out, is the human predicament. Although most of us do not directly cause these inequalities by taking food away from poor children or actively creating handicaps or disabilities, the knowledge that we live in an interconnected world shot through with inequality calls us to a certain responsibility. As Birch and Cobb write, "A community becomes responsible for the deprived through every responsible member of that community. This is the strong meaning of justice. Justice does not require equality. It does require that we share one another's fate."[11] In other words, we have a duty to help others achieve their highest potential for rich experience and creativity.

An acceptance of our fates as separate and yet interconnected, equal and yet unequal, also asks that we recognize the wide variety of

---

11. Ibid., page 165.

ways in which richness of experience may be made manifest. One person's garbage is another person's gold. No one person or culture can be said to reliably achieve the greatest richness of experience at all times. Even agreeing on when these moments of value are manifested is an area for fruitful interpersonal and cross-cultural discussion. In the construction of ethical norms, diversity confers a real advantage. We can, and should, learn from one another. As theologian Jurgen Moltmann writes, "We do not wish to know so that we can dominate. We desire to know in order to participate. This kind of knowledge confers community, and can be termed communicative knowledge, as compared with dominating knowledge. It lets life be life and cherishes its livingness."[12]

The nascent world of cyberspace opens vast new potential for ethical action in the world. Most people would characterize computers as having only instrumental value. They are a means to an end, the end being the uses we humans put them to. But that characterization reduces the potential of cyberspace as a medium coexisting with our divine creativity. The world of cyberspace does have intrinsic value; it does exhibit some small measure of richness of experience. From feedback loops to neural networks, evolving software and agents that learn, digital processes are exhibiting some ability to respond to and participate in their environment. The richness of experience that this produces is located not in the hardware boxes that we think of as computers but in the dynamic, creative unfolding that forms the soul of cyberspace.

At this point in the evolution of cyberspace, its intrinsic value remains small. It may always be so, but the recognition of it serves to remind us of the ways in which cyberspace is of a piece with the larger

---

12. Jurgen Moltmann, *God and Creation: An Ecological Doctrine of Creation*, London: SCM Press, 1985, page 32.

universe, actively participating in its creative, spiritual evolution. At the same time, cyberspace has enormous instrumental value contained in its ability to increase dramatically the richness of experience in the human and nonhuman worlds. Cyberspace offers a new lens through which we can grasp the enormous diversity of creative expression evolving throughout the universe. Cyberspace enables us to connect with one another in new ways, expanding our understanding of justice, equality, and human and environmental rights. These are important attributes that must be considered when we think about the role cyberspace has to play in spiritual evolution. When we guide cyberspace from a place of theological and ethical reflection, we further not only our richness of experience but that of the universe as a whole.

SEVERED HEADS

The art of ethical living continually forms and reforms who we are and how we conceive of the world. Like theological inquiry and faith, ethics is a journey without end that engages the whole of who we are. Ethics begins as a response to our unique, bodily based awareness. This experience is then filtered through our historical and cultural understandings of right and wrong in a complex blending of subjective and objective truths. When we act, we communicate a moral stance. As we observe our actions, we learn more about the moral stance that we have communicated. And back and forth we go.

Moral action is ultimately a deeply personal issue, born from self-knowledge embedded in our bodies, history, culture, community, values, and faith. Yet, ethically guided activity takes place in and has deep consequences for the communities in which we live. How then do we as individuals further richness of experience? Philosopher Mark John-son argues that the "moral imagination"[13] offers one of our most pow-erful tools in this quest. Through moral imagination we employ an "imaginative rationality," a faculty that enables us to blend our subjec-tive experiences and insights with an objective, rational sense of right and wrong. The result is not a rigid set of rules that tells us what to do, but a dynamic set of values that can evolve along with a changing world.

According to Johnson, the second wave of empirical research in the field of cognitive science underscores the fact that imagination is one of the central faculties that enables us to enact our moral beliefs. This research reveals that objective rules have very little to do with how we ultimately choose to act in the world. Instead, we come to understand the world through a series of bodily based experiences framed in terms of semantics, narrative, prototypes, and metaphor. In other words, it is the stories that we tell and our interpretations of them that stimulate us to act.

Of the various tactics we use, metaphors are the primary way in which we access and employ our moral imaginations. At first glance, this idea may strike us as unstable. How can we build moral lives on metaphors and seemingly emotional, impressionistic expressions of imagination? But as Johnson argues, metaphors are hardly unstable. They can best be understood as the articulation of our shared experi-ence. In this way, metaphors—such as the desktops through which we view cyberspace—offer a common cultural platform for discussion that goes deeper than focusing solely on an objective set of abstract, ratio-nal laws.

Johnson argues that the fatal flaw of the objective moral approach

---

13. Mark Johnson, *Moral Imagination*.

is the assumption that we are rational beings capable of acting on a set of universal laws based on moral reason. This view locks moral deliberation into a series of frozen objectives, losing any sense of ethical life as a process of change and growth. To complicate matters further, objective moral laws often function well only in certain, prototypical situations. Real life doesn't often fit these neat categories. Our most difficult moral decisions are those that fall outside the boundaries of objective moral laws.

But the theory of moral laws doesn't have it all wrong. We need guidance from moral principles and ideals in order to act. The problem arises in the difficulty of mapping these principles directly onto the complex fabric of our lives. In practice, we weave moral laws into the unfolding narrative of our lives through metaphor and imagination. As Johnson writes, "The crux of this view of moral criticism as fundamentally imaginative is that moral objectivity consists, not in having an absolute 'God's-eye point of view,' but rather in a specific kind of reflective, exploratory, and critical process of evaluation carried out through communal discourse and practice."[14]

Imagination is the human faculty that enables us to envision possibility. With it, we can sort through a myriad of complex alternatives, using moral ideals as our guide, to find appropriate courses of action. Analysis of the metaphors we use can offer deep insight into the nature of our values and their location in our experience. Certain metaphors come from our bodily experience while others have cultural grounding. For example, the metaphor of "desktop" as an interface to cyberspace reveals a moral imperative to work, to order our information in a certain way, and to increase productivity, thereby becoming more useful members of our society. At a deeper level, this metaphor creates a space

---

14. Ibid., page 217.

optimized for intellectual experience, resulting in a disembodied world best suited, to use Brenda Laurel's term, to "severed heads." Char Davies's Osmose, on the other hand, utilizes a set of metaphors taken from nature as the interface to the cyberworld. This set of metaphors supports an ethic of deep connection to the body and the natural world.

Metaphors have an enormously important role to play in our ethical evolution with cyberspace. Metaphors are the primary currency we use to access the digital world. In this context, the moral content of the metaphors we use in cyberspace carry additional weight. For example, the metaphor of pages that guides the vast and rapidly growing WWW is born of a complex set of assumptions that have direct ethical implications. Perhaps the most basic assumption is access itself. The life of the Web tacitly assumes a certain level of computer literacy and access among its participants. For most of us who live a life connected to the wired world, the lives of the billions of people who have never even touched a computer rarely cross our screens of awareness. The implications of this small example, hidden behind every click of the Web, are staggering.

Our current interface options more accurately reflect the scientific and corporate forces that develop computers than the potential of the medium itself. Two-dimensional, objective interfaces optimized for fast and productive completion of business tasks such as writing letters, sending e-mail, calculating budgets, and preparing presentations are what people think of when they think about computers. These interfaces, along with the newer electronic brochure-cum-banner style of the WWW, serve to reduce cyberspace to a tool for business productivity.

Cyberspace can't be reduced to a business tool or even a radically new communications medium. It is what we imagine it to be, reflecting the intentions and values that we bring to its design, deployment, and implementation. This realization brings with it both promise and deep responsibility. When we push the metaphoric potential of cyberspace in new directions, a dialectic with the digital is engaged that helps to reveal what Carol Gigliotti, an artist and ethicist, calls the "moral content of our desires, needs and our plans." Perhaps the most powerful and hopeful of these metaphors is found in the interactivity of cyberspace.

The metaphor of interaction has the greatest potential for creating a moral environment of empowering the participant. When this interactivity is reduced to mere consumption, we do ourselves and the medium a disservice. Instead, the interface should seek to create a metaphor of *responsiveness,* a stance that communicates the moral values of relationship, community, and empathy. As Gigliotti writes, "Ultimately, the interface must reflect—since it will also direct—our sense of wholeness as physical beings and our trust in our ability to make judgments."[15] The responsiveness of cyberspace can act as a powerful stimulation for the development of moral imagination.

Gigliotti argues that this interactive aesthetic of wholeness should be extended into the *content* of the digital experience. Content should be defined by the participants and be responsive to the context of their physical situation. In this sense, the digital and the organic can become dynamically engaged through the experience of the participant. This same responsiveness should also hold true for the environment created by the digital world and the way in which the participant perceives it. The participant's experience should be reflected in the environment itself, and he or she should be able to choose the senses desired to engage it. The empowerment of the individual and his or her ability to reach new levels of personal insight are greatly enhanced when these aspects of the interface remain interactive.

---

15. Carol Gigliotti, "Aesthetics of a Virtual World," page 294.

The importance of embodied wisdom can never be far from our thinking when it comes to creating morally sound experiences of cyberspace. For cyberspace to have deep meaning and importance, it must coexist with the organic world in which we reside. In order to achieve this, Gigliotti argues that it must be clear how our actions in the digital are affecting others both in the virtual world and outside of it. The digital world should also be moldable and able to push back at the participant. This "push" doesn't mean a stream of uninvited advertising, but refers to the fact that the physical reality in which the participant is located should exert some influence on his or her experience in the virtual world. Through metaphors such as interactivity, plasticity, and permeability, we can begin to formulate experiences of the digital that lead to enhanced moral experience.

Cyberspace offers us a new palette on which to manifest the life-enhancing values that move us toward ever greater richness of experience—love, connection, justice, empathy, care, equality, and responsibility. This will happen only if we consciously work to create implementations and experiences of the medium that reflect these moral injunctions. Understanding that cyberspace has some intrinsic value that ties it irretrievably to the larger sacred fabric of the universe forms an important starting point. With this perspective firmly in hand, our instrumental use of the medium becomes enriched and enlivened by the knowledge that it is an expression of divine spirit working to enhance the richness of experience of all creation. Through our creative process and our moral imagination, we not only bring the spark of divine spirit into our lives but open the possibility of working with cyberspace to further spiritual evolution.

SPiRiT iN ACTiON

On February 8, 1996, the monks of the Namgyal Monastery, the personal monastery of the Dalai Lama, performed a blessing of cyberspace. In a summary of the blessing available at the monastery's Web site, the following appeared: "Tibetan Buddhism, known for its mastery of the mind, has an area of concentration called 'tantra' that specializes in bringing spiritual motivation to the realm of mental projections. In using the Internet we noticed the Net breeds both positive and negative behaviors, reflecting the very human nature of we who use it. In this sense it became apparent that the space known as cyberspace was very appropriate for a tantric spiritual blessing—to help purify how it is used and the 'results' it yields."[16]

To perform the blessing, the monks turned to the Kalachakra Tantra as a vehicle. This particular tantra focuses on space and consciousness as one of the primary elements of the universe. According to the monks, cyberspace has certain qualities in common with ordinary space, which they see as "the absence of obstructions," something that cannot be seen or measured but nonetheless can be understood and utilized as a field for mental activity. During the thirty-minute ceremony, the monks chanted from the Kalachakra "while envisioning space as cyberspace, the networked realm of computers, in their imagination. An image of the Kalachakra mandala, actually a scanned photo of a sand painting made earlier by the monks, was present on a computer as a visual aid, but was not considered essential to the power of the blessing." The monks of the Namgyal Monastery plan to undertake more blessings of cyberspace in the future.

---

16. See http://www.namgyal.org/blessing.html

The Buddhists are not the only organized religion on-line. Every major religion, and hundreds of smaller ones, are present on the Net. Cyber churches, temples, and sanghas can be found by the dozen. In these environs, people meet, argue, pray, and commune with one another. Charles Henderson, a Presbyterian minister and founder of the First Church of Cyberspace, points out that "one can move with stunning speed from the Cathedral of St. John the Divine to a topless bar; one can work out one's astrological chart, converse with a witch, correspond with Newt Gingrich, or join in prayer with a monastic community in France. . . . While wandering from one site to another, we can spin from the creative chaos of the Internet a web of our own. Within its constantly changing dimensions, we can give shape and substance to the interior life."[17]

The community life that is emerging in cyberspace has an enormous range of expression. In addition to experiences that are overtly religious in nature, there are a myriad of examples of the medium enabling social and political change in service of the disadvantaged, of other species, and of the environment. John Young claims that the on-line discussion groups (known as ListServs) have had an enormous impact on grassroots political organizations. Young commented, "ListServs allow people to have an ongoing conversation about their own organizing, to pass along fast-breaking information as it happens, and to coordinate campaigns almost up to the minute. For example, if you are with a forest group in rural Montana, and you want to network with people in Alaska, Idaho, British Columbia, Oregon, and Washington about regional forest-management issues, there is just no way you are going to have the money to bring people together for physical

---

17. Charles Henderson, "The Future of ARIL in the Information Age," *Cross Currents*, summer 1996, page 192.

meetings. This technology really makes that possible in a way that even the telephone system couldn't."

In its current incarnation, artists are creating some of the most powerful instances of sacred cyberspace. Leslie Huppert has undertaken a project called The Robe, which creates a deep marriage between the cyber and the organic. For this work, Huppert widely disseminated over the Net an invitation for people to send her bits of fabric that had meaning for them. She requested that the fabric be accompanied by a story. She plans to take the fabric and build a huge meditation tent from it, filled with the stories. Simultaneously, participants will be able to access the stories as well as the responses of those in The Robe on the Web.

Ebon Fisher, a multimedia artist and former teacher at MIT's Media Lab, has been exploring another form of cyber creativity. For the last year, Fisher's cyber manifesto, which he calls Wigglism, has been circulating on the Internet, evolving and growing as people attach comments and ideas to it. Fisher writes, "The essence of the project is to abandon the discourse of 'art' (a humanist creature) and redefine cultural activity as an act of coilings, creating vital lifeforms. . . . We nurture that which wiggles—of flesh or steel, sinew or circuit, mud or imagination; transmuting art into a zoology of spirit." The manifesto reads, in part, "We dissolve every bloodless workstation, artifact, and module of consumption, into the acids of living ritual. We grow connections in an ecology of twitches and presences; soaking tendrils of thought and conscience in a spray of fibrous feedback; infusing phantoms and facts with equal measures of visceral significance; writhing among the rivulets and curls of screaming knowledge. . . . We struggle to love these creatures, these convulsions, to keep that which is lively, and that which sustains life, in supreme focus."[18]

---

18. See Wigglism at http://www.artnetweb.com/port/wigglism

However many creative uses of cyberspace can be found—and there are many—they remain in the minority. The reasons for this are manifold, having to do with the relative youth of the medium, the social and historical forces that gave it birth, and the current business models that dominate its development and deployment. If we wish to further the use of cyberspace in the service of rich experience, we need to approach it with a new set of clearly stated intentions. It is my hope that there will be many conversations about how best to evolve this unique medium in the service of moral and spiritual growth leading to ethical action. It is only in the context of communal reflection that the sacred dimension of cyberspace will truly flourish. To help this process along its way, I offer the following five concepts as evocative but not prescriptive guides.

//   **Pursue Connection.** Connection must be striven for at all times. Connection in this case refers not only to connection between people—which is of course to be pursued—but connection between us and the divine in its many guises. Connection also refers to the importance of permeability between the organic and the digital. The powerful dynamic between the two worlds must always be carefully and consciously nurtured.

//   **Foster Diversity.** Diversity serves as one of the primary pillars of rich experience. It is from the multitudes that we learn about ourselves. Cyberspace has a unique role to play as it ties us together in global experience. We must always seek to guard against "electronic colonialism" or the homogenization of culture into one particular viewpoint. Cyberspace can be a powerful tool in the fostering of diversity; it is up to us to guide it in this direction.

//   Be Understood in Context. Cyberspace does not exist in a vacuum. It is a part of the global ecosystem. As such, it is imperative that we consider the systemic effects of technology before we implement it. Whom will it help? Whom will it hurt? What are the short- and long-term ramifications? Questions such as these must become standard in our technology assessment.

//   Be Driven by Clear Intention. One of the most important things that we can do to protect against the ill effects of cyberspace is to guide it with clear, spiritual intention. This requires that we go inside ourselves and develop self-knowledge. Self-knowledge is the basis of spiritual insight and evolution. As we come to know our values, our morals, our deepest beliefs, and our areas of pain and suffering, we gain clarity into how divine creativity is working through our lives. With this understanding we can form concrete intentions for guiding our actions in the world.

//   Nurture Creativity. Creativity forms the heart of spiritual evolution. Creativity in service of enhanced rich experience for the whole of creation is the core idea that guides the living of a spiritual life. Whenever cyberspace furthers positive creativity in this sense, it furthers spiritual evolution. We must cast our hearts, minds, and imaginations widely into the sphere of cyberspace, praying that we may continually discover new applications of the digital that enhance this absolutely fundamental dynamic.

We are evolution's self-reflective face. Through us—thinking, feeling, embodied creatures—the evolutionary force of divine creativity has found self-conscious awareness. Along with this enormous power comes an awesome and, at times, mind-numbing responsibility. Whether we are aware of it or not, we are shaping the direction of the universe at a very deep level. At this highly charged point in history, computers have emerged, offering a new set of potentials and challenges. Through the power of computation, the universal spirit of divine creativity is extending into a new terrain. It is when this knowledge comes fully into our conscious awareness that our deeper journey with cyberspace will truly have begun. May we travel in the wisdom of divine spirit and self-knowledge.

(BIBLIOGRAPHY)

Abraham, Ralph. *Chaos, Gaia, Eros*. San Francisco: HarperSanFrancisco, 1994.

Adams, Carol J. (ed). *Ecofeminism and the Sacred*. New York: Continuum, 1993.

Aukstakalnis, Steve, and David Blatner. *Silicon Mirage: The Art and Science of Virtual Reality*. Berkeley: Peachpit Press, 1992.

Barbour, Ian. *Ethics in an Age of Technology: The Gifford Lectures, Volume Two*. San Francisco: HarperSanFrancisco, 1990–1991.

———. *Religion in an Age of Science: The Gifford Lectures, Volume One*. San Francisco: HarperSanFrancisco, 1989–1990.

Becker, Ernest. *The Denial of Death*. New York: The Free Press, 1973.

Benedikt, Michael (ed). *Cyberspace: First Steps*. Cambridge, Massachusetts: MIT Press, 1992.

Birch, Charles. *A Purpose for Everything: Religion in a Postmodern Worldview*. Mystic, Connecticut: Twenty-Third Publications, 1990.

Birch, Charles, and John B. Cobb, Jr. *The Liberation of Life: From the Cell to the Community*. Denton, Texas: Environmental Ethics Books, 1990.

Birch, Charles, William Eakin, and Jay B. McDaniel (eds.). *Liberating Life: Contemporary Approaches to Ecological Theology*. Maryknoll, New York: Orbis Books, 1990.

Borgmann, Albert. *Technology and the Character of Contemporary Life: A Philosophical Inquiry.* Chicago: University of Chicago Press, 1984.

Brand, Stewart. *The Media Lab: Inventing the Future at M.I.T.* New York: Penguin Books, 1987.

Chalmers, David J. *The Conscious Mind: In Search of a Fundamental Theory.* New York: Oxford University Press, 1996.

Cobb, John B., Jr. "Natural Causality and Divine Action." *Idealistic Studies* 3, 1973, pp. 207–22.

Crevier, Daniel. *AI: The Tumultuous History of the Search for Artificial Intelligence.* New York: Basic Books, 1993.

Davies, Char. "Osmose: Notes on 'Being' in Immersive Virtual Space." Unpublished notes.

Davies, Paul. *The Mind of God.* New York: Simon & Schuster, 1992.

De Landa, Manuel. *War in the Age of Intelligent Machines.* New York: Zone Books, 1991.

Diamond, Irene, and Gloria Feman Orenstein (eds.). *Reweaving the World: The Emergence of Ecofeminism.* San Francisco: Sierra Club Books, 1990.

de Duve, Christian. *Vital Dust: Life as a Cosmic Imperative.* New York: Basic Books, 1995.

Dyson, Freeman. *Infinite in All Directions.* New York: Harper & Row, 1988.

Forrest, Stephanie (ed.). *Emergent Computation.* Cambridge, Massachusetts: MIT Press, 1991.

Gibson, William. *Neuromancer.* New York: Ace Books, 1984.

Gigliotti, Carol. "Aesthetics of a Virtual World." *Leonardo* 28, no. 4, 1995, pp. 289–95.

Gopnik, Adam. "The Virtual Bishop." *The New Yorker,* March 18, 1996.

Gore, Al. *Earth in the Balance: Ecology and the Human Spirit,* Boston: Houghton Mifflin, 1992.

Griffin, David Ray. *God & Religion in the Postmodern World.* Albany, New York: State University of New York Press, 1989.

Griffin, Susan. *The Eros of Everyday Life: Essays on Ecology, Gender and Society.* New York: Doubleday, 1995.

Grim, John and Mary Evelyn. *Teilhard de Chardin: A Short Biography.* Teilhard Studies, no. 11, spring 1984. Chambersburg, PA.

Haraway, Donna J. *Simians, Cyborgs, and Women: The Reinvention of Nature.* New York: Routledge, 1991.

Hayward, Jeremy. *Perceiving Ordinary Magic: Science & Intuitive Wisdom.* Boston: Shambhala, 1984.

Heim, Michael. *The Metaphysics of Virtual Reality.* Oxford: Oxford University Press, 1993.

Hillis, W. Daniel. "What is Massively Parallel Computing, and Why Is It Important?" *Daedalus,* winter 1992, pp. 1–15.

Jahn, Robert G., and Brenda J. Dunne. *Margins of Reality: The Role of Consciousness in the Physical World.* New York: Harcourt Brace & Company, 1987.

Johnson, Mark. *The Body in the Mind: The Bodily Basis of Meaning, Imagination, and Reason.* Chicago: University of Chicago Press, 1987.

———. *Moral Imagination: Implications of Cognitive Science for Ethics.* Chicago: University of Chicago Press, 1993.

Kauffman, Stuart. *At Home in the Universe: The Search for Laws of Self-Organization and Complexity.* Oxford: Oxford University Press, 1995.

Kelly, Kevin. *Out of Control: The Rise of Neo-biological Civilization.* Reading, Massachusetts: Addison-Wesley, 1994.

Koestler, Arthur. *The Act of Creation.* New York: Dell Publishing, 1964.

Kuhn, Thomas. *The Structure of Scientific Revolutions,* second edition. Chicago: University of Chicago Press, 1970.

Laurel, Brenda. Panel, "Computer Graphics—Are We Forcing People to Evolve?" from SIGGRAPH '94, Orlando, Florida. Available at: http://www.tauzero.com/Brenda_Laurel/Severed_Heads

———. *Computers as Theatre.* Reading, Massachusetts: Addison-Wesley, 1991.

Laurel, Brenda, Rachel Strickland, and Rob Tow. "Placeholder: Landscape and Narrative in Virtual Environments." *ACM Computer Graphics Quarterly* 28, no. 2, May 1994.

Levy, Steven. *Artificial Life: A Report from the Frontier Where Computers Meet Biology.* New York: Vintage Books, 1992.

Lukas, Ellen and Mary. *Teilhard: A Biography.* London, 1977.

Maes, Pattie. "Modeling Adaptive Autonomous Agents." *Artificial Life* 1, 1994, pp. 135–62.

McFague, Sallie. *The Body of God: An Ecological Theology.* Minneapolis: Fortress Press, 1993.

Merchant, Carolyn. *The Death of Nature: Women, Ecology and the Scientific Revolution.* San Francisco: HarperSanFrancisco, 1990.

Miles, Margaret R. *The Fullness of Life: Historical Foundations for a New Asceticism.* Philadelphia: The Westminster Press, 1981.

Murray, Janet H. *Hamlet on the Holodeck: The Future of Narrative in Cyberspace.* New York: The Free Press, 1997.

Ong, Walter J. *Orality & Literacy: The Technologizing of the Word.* London and New York: Routledge, 1982.

Percy, Walker. *Lost in the Cosmos: The Last Self-help Book.* New York: Farrar, Straus & Giroux, 1983.

Postman, Neil. *Technopoly: The Surrender of Culture to Technology.* New York: Alfred A. Knopf, 1992.

Rasmussen, Larry L. *Moral Fragments & Moral Community: A Proposal for Church and Society*. Minneapolis: Fortress Press, 1993.

Ray, Thomas S. "Artificial Life." Available at: http://www.hip.atr.co.jp/~ray/

———. "An Evolutionary Approach to Synthetic Biology: Zen and the Art of Creating Life." *Artificial Life* 1, 1994, pp. 179–209.

Rich, Adrienne. *Of Woman Born*. New York: Bantam Books, 1976.

Romanyshyn, Robert D. *Technology as Symptom and Dream*. London and New York: Routledge, 1989.

Rothenberg, David. *Hand's End: Technology and the Limits of Nature*. Berkeley: University of California Press, 1993.

Rushkoff, Douglas. *Cyberia: Life in the Trenches of Hyperspace*. San Francisco: HarperSanFrancisco, 1995.

Santmire, H. Paul. *The Travail of Nature: The Ambiguous Ecological Promise of Christian Theology*. Philadelphia: Fortress Press, 1985.

Spitz, Rejane. "Qualitative, Dialectical and Experiential Domains of Electronic Art." *Leonardo* 28, no. 4, 1995, pp. 319–23.

Stephenson, Neal. *Snowcrash*. New York: Bantam Books, 1993.

Tawney, R. H. *Religion and the Rise of Capitalism*. New York: Harcourt Brace & Co., 1926.

Teilhard de Chardin, Pierre. *The Divine Milieu*. New York: Harper & Row, 1965.

———. *The Phenomenon of Man*. New York: Harper & Row, 1965.

Turkle, Sherry. *Life on the Screen: Identity in the Age of the Internet*. New York: Simon & Schuster, 1995.

———. *The Second Self: Computers and the Human Spirit*. New York: Simon & Schuster, 1984.

Varela, Francisco J., Evan Thompson, and Eleanor Rosch. *The Embodied Mind: Cognitive Science and Human Experience*. Cambridge, Massachusetts: MIT Press, 1993.

Waldrop, M. Mitchell. *Complexity: The Emerging Science at the Edge of Order and Chaos.* New York: Simon & Schuster, 1992.

Weber, Max. *The Protestant Ethic and the Spirit of Capitalism.* New York: Charles Scribner's Sons, 1958.

Whitehead, Alfred North. *Adventures of Ideas.* New York: The Free Press, 1933.

———. *Process and Reality.* New York: The Free Press, 1978.

Wilber, Ken. *Eye to Eye: The Quest for the New Paradigm.* Boston: Shambhala, 1990.

———. *Sex, Ecology, Spirituality: The Spirit of Evolution.* Boston: Shambhala, 1995.

Wilber, Ken, Jack Engler, and Daniel P. Brown. *Transformations of Consciousness.* Boston: Shambhala, 1986.

Wolpert, Julian. "Center Cities as Havens and Traps for Low-Income Communities: The Potential Impact of Advanced Information Technology." Session summary, February 21, 1996, Colloquium on Advanced Information Technology, Low-Income Communities, and the City, Department of Urban Studies and Planning, M.I.T. Paper available at: http://sap.mit.edu/projects/colloquium/

Woolley, Benjamin. *Virtual Worlds: A Journey in Hype and Hyperreality,* Oxford: Blackwell Publishers, 1992.

Wright, Richard. "The Image in Art and 'Computer Art.' " *Leonardo,* Supplemental Issue, 1989.

Wright, Robert. *Three Scientists and Their Gods:* New York: Times Books, 1988.

Young, John E. "Global Network: Computers in a Sustainable Society." *Worldwatch Paper* 115. Washington, D.C.: Worldwatch Institute, 1993.

Zimmerman, Michael E. *Contesting Earth's Future: Radical Ecology and Postmodernity.* Berkeley: University of California Press, 1994.

(A C K N O W L E D G M E N T S)

No book is solely the expression of one person. Countless people have contributed to the evolution of these ideas, in ways both big and small. Insight, friendship, community, intellectual and spiritual sustenance—all of these are born of connection with others. Over the years, many people have helped guide my thinking, offered support and reassurance, and given me the courage to move forward. Without their generosity, this book would simply not have been possible.

I am particularly grateful to Larry Rasmussen at Union Theological Seminary, and to John Cobb, David Ray Griffin, and Granville Henry at the Claremont Colleges for their theological insight and guidance. I must thank those in the world of technology who shared their time and thoughts with me, including Char Davies, Tom Ray, Kevin Kelly, Brenda Laurel, Robert Jahn, Brenda Dunne, Ralph Abraham, and Patty Maes. I would also like to thank John Perry Barlow for his early encouragement.

No list of thanks would be complete without a heartfelt expression of gratitude to my editor, Karen Rinaldi, to Lara Webb, and to my agent, Melanie Jackson. All three signed on early and enthusiastically to this project, and then read and reread drafts of the manuscript, offering guidance and suggestions at key junctures.

Among my friends and family, I must thank in particular Simone Otus, Chris Clyne, Rebecca Perl, Andrea Chapin, Virginia Chapin, Andre Carothers, Melissa Cobb, and Mary Cobb, who were always there with a supportive word, cheering me on. The unswerving belief my parents have in me, even when it seems most unfounded, has built a firm foundation in my life. To them I am grateful. My children, Jeremiah and Samuel, whose incandescent minds and spirits bring such richness and depth to the world, remind me daily of what is really important. Without them, much in these pages would lose its force. And finally I must thank my husband, Joel Kreisberg, for living through the continual highs and lows that punctuate the life of the writer. His critical insight, understanding, and sense of humor were invaluable throughout.

(I N D E X)

(A)

Abraham, Ralph, 46–48
agency, 10, 11, 102, 103, 178–84
AL (artificial life), 159–61
algorithms, 21, 33, 51, 155
Andreesson, Mark, 47
artificial intelligence (AI), 166–72,
  175, 178
artificial life (AL), 158–61, 164,
  166, 180
ascent, metaphor of, 24–26
asceticism, 201–5
atheism, scientific, 28
attention epistemology, 211
augmented intelligence, 177–85
Augustine, Saint, 173
autonomous agents, 178–84

(B)

Bachelard, Gaston, 198
Barlow, John Perry, 85, 92
Belgrade unrest, 212–14
Bergson, Henri, 80
biosphere, 99–100, 106, 119
Birch, Charles, 182–83, 222–26
bodily wisdom, 188–92, 200–204,
  206–9

Bohr, Niels, 140, 141
bottom-up programming, 165–72,
  175–77, 179, 182–84
Buber, Martin, 146
Burners-Lee, Tim, 47
Burtt, Edwin, 27–28

(C)

Calder, Alexander, 49–50
Calvin, John, 25–26
chance, in evolution, 36–40, 83, 88,
  162, 163, 183
chaos theory, 32, 48
Chavez, Anthony, 181
chess, 1–7, 12–13, 14
circular causality, 61
Cobb, John B., Jr., 53–58, 69, 70,
  123, 175, 182–83, 209, 222–26
coevolutionary process, 20
collective, of autonomous agents,
  178–83
complexity, 90, 96, 155, 157, 158,
  161, 164, 168, 169
complexity-consciousness, law of,
  82–83, 109, 114
compression, force of, 87–88, 93